50 SUCCESSFUL SWARTHMORE APPLICATION ESSAYS

William Han
Sean Cheng

Paperback edition: ISBN 978-1-7356867-0-7

Kindle edition: ISBN 978-1-7356867-1-4

First edition
November 2020

For details on how to seek permission, please email
swarthmoreessays@gmail.com.

Trademark notice: Product or corporate names may be trademarks

Cover design by: William Han
Library of Congress Control Number: 2018675309
Printed in the United States of America

To Our Parents For Always Being Our Number One Supporters

CONTENTS

Title Page

Copyright

Dedication

Preface   1

I. Essay-Writing Advice   5

II. Swarthmore Admissions Officer Q&A   26

III. Your Written Tour of Swarthmore   31

IV. THE ESSAYS   43

Common Application Essays   44

QuestBridge Essays   112

Why Swarthmore Essays   141

Our Essays   185

Transfer Essay   192

Acknowledgement   199

PREFACE

Each school evaluates a candidate's college application differently. Some focus more on grades and test scores, while others care more about the personality/essay of the applicant. Swarthmore is a very particular kind of school with a strong personality (see Your Written Tour of Swarthmore), so it would make sense for admissions officers to pay special attention to the applicant's essays to evaluate whether or not the student would thrive in such an environment. That's why one of the goals of this book is to help students see for themselves what kinds of essays/students Swarthmore likes to admit, and thus 1) help them judge whether or not they are a fit for Swarthmore and 2) help them craft great essays that cater to Swarthmore specifically.

We also want to emphasize that while Swarthmore is a one-of-a-kind learning environment with fantastic opportunities, it is not the ideal school for everyone. The college application process is a bit like dating. It can be tempting to just apply to as many schools as possible with the hopes of getting into one (like desperately looking for a significant other), but we encourage you to think deeply before applying to a school— after all it's going to be a four year long marriage. We hope our chapter on Swarthmore and the stories in the following essays will help you make a more informed decision on whether or not to apply there.

Perhaps our greatest motivation for putting this book together was to provide high school students from socioeconomically disadvantaged backgrounds with a helpful guide for applying to a school that is quite generous with financial aid. Over half of Swarthmore's student body received financial aid in 2018-2019. Swarthmore is a cash-free campus, meaning there are no "additional fees" for daily life at Swarthmore— movie nights, laundry, printing, athletic events, and even transportation to and from the nearest Target, movie theatre, and mall are all free. Moreover, Swarthmore has a generous budget for activities. It subsidizes transportation to and from conferences, hackathons, and other events. Countless clubs are awarded generous budgets to perform and compete all around the east coast. Once a year, it even equips groups of 4 random Swarthmore students with train tickets, $25, and a notebook to have an adventure in Philadelphia. Additionally, Swarthmore pays for admitted students from low-income and first generation backgrounds to visit Swarthmore each Spring (SwatLight). The college also funds summer internships and research through the Lang Center so that students can be free to pursue an unpaid internship, non-profit/volunteer work, or research during the summer.

Unfortunately, when we tell people we attend Swarthmore college, most people stare blankly at us because they've never heard of it. We wanted to increase awareness about Swarthmore in the communities that would benefit most from a Swarthmore education, and provide a resource that would help students in those communities have the best chance at a Swarthmore acceptance. Most students from low-income/first-generation backgrounds can't afford college counseling, and generally lack access to guidance in an increasingly complex college application process. In addition, many students can't afford to go on college tours across the country to experience a school firsthand and get a sense of whether or not they would be a good fit there. We hope that this book can provide some direction on writing the "Why Swarthmore" essay, and give readers a sense of what a strong Common Application essay looks like. After all, one of the best ways to learn how to write a great essay is to learn by example.

We also wanted this book to provide timely help, as COVID-19 has changed the application process quite suddenly. SATs and ACTs are no longer required at many schools, so essays will play a much more significant role in the screening process. In light of the new emphasis on essays and qualitative aspects of the application, we believe that the impact of this book will be magnified.

We hope these essays inspire you and help you produce a superb essay of your own. That said, originality is key to writing a phenomenal essay. We can't emphasize this enough. If a friend or loved one can read your essay and immediately recognize exactly who wrote it, you know you've hit the mark. Also, there is no such thing as a "model" essay. One thing you'll notice is that each essay in this book is different. Each person has their own story, and the goal of the writer should be to bring out that story in its best form. That looks different for each person. Admissions officers are trying to learn about you, so trying to copy the format or style of an essay defeats the whole purpose. However, great essays often share common characteristics, and in this book we hope to help shed light on what those qualities are so that your essay can also have those elements. While there is no such thing as a "perfect" or "model" essay, there is such thing as a relatively good or bad essay, and writing a good essay requires skill and effort.

Another myth we want to dispel is the following: "if you write a perfect essay (like one you may hope to find in this book), you will get into a school like Swarthmore." Remember that the essay is just one part of the application. Applications with great essays get rejected, and applications with bad essays get accepted. The essay isn't everything. But, of course, you still want to write the best essay you can to maximize your chances of admission. We'll talk more about that in the "Essay-writing Advice" chapter.

All in all, we wanted to write this book to help you write the best possible essay you can, and to help your essays become "Successful Swarthmore Essays" themselves. Best of luck.

Sincerely,

Will and Sean

I. ESSAY-WRITING ADVICE

Outline:
1.   Intro
2.   Key Essay Qualities for Liberal Arts Applications
3.   How to Begin
4.   The PAR Framework
5.   Common Essay Mistakes
6.   How Important is the Personal Statement?
7.   The Why Swarthmore Essay

The Personal Statement. It's a daunting task, attempting to sift through an entire lifetime of experiences to determine what to write about. How can I stand out? What topics should I choose? How can I best showcase my personality? All of these questions are important to answer when it comes to writing a terrific essay. We hope that we can help answer them in this chapter.

The personal statement is the one part of the application that you have complete and direct control over. If you are a senior, you are probably not able to change your SAT score or your GPA at this point, so it is not worth stressing over any of these things. But, you do have full power over every letter in your personal statement, so investing time and effort into your essay is the best way to increase your chances of admission.

It's natural to feel a growing sense of pressure with that amount of control. But don't worry! We've got you covered. Let's start by answering a question that will help inform almost any essay decision you can make — what are the key qualities for liberal arts application essays?

Key Essay Qualities for Liberal Arts Applications

It's hard to know exactly what to include in your personal statement if you don't know why you should or shouldn't include it. Should you write about this experience or that one? Should you cut this detail out of the essay, or not? Each possibility in these writing decisions will showcase different things about you. So which should you choose?

That depends largely on what you believe admissions officers care about. What do they want to hear from you? This fundamental question should underlie every decision you make about your essay. You don't want to write blindly. It's worth taking some time to figure out what your audience cares about and get into the heads of the admissions committee a little bit. Luckily for you, we've done some of that work for you: make sure to read through our Swarthmore Admissions Officer Q&A chapter. Below, we've outlined a few more things that are particularly important for liberal arts colleges, and why. Many of these points are generalizable to other types of schools as well.

Interesting to Read

For one, liberal arts colleges care that your essay is interesting to read. Admissions officers read hundreds of applications a day. It will help you tremendously if your essays are stimulating and at least a little creative. It is especially important to do this in your intro, where you want to hook your reader and draw them in. Here is a small list of ways you can do this, with example essays that you can find in this book:

1) Have a sense of humor. There is no better way to make your essay fun to read than to write something that will make your readers laugh. Examples: "Food is a Celebration of Our Blessings," "One Cent Please" (in Additionals), "Tangents"

2) Put imagery and sensory details in your story to draw your reader into the scene of your experience. Example: "No Beard for Now," "A Song of Love"

3) Try to include any tidbits of personality you possibly can. Maybe it's a nickname you had for someone (perhaps in another language), or a nickname someone had for you. Maybe it's that you love spicy food, or hate wearing a specific article of clothing. Examples: "You Need to Chili," "Reflection on Family Conflict"

4) Include interesting details. Perhaps you did an activity in high school that was obscure and relatively unknown, or is rich with details that are fascinating or weird. Mentioning these details will enrich the story and add flavor to your essay. Example: "To Punch the Way of the Teacher," "Discovering My Perspective"

5) Write insightful reflections. Incorporating some eloquent and original thoughts into your essay will impress your reader. There are some essays in this book that will make you think, "wow, I've never thought about that before." An essay that presents a

new and fresh take or has profound reflections will show that the writer is the type of thinker that liberal arts colleges would love to admit. Example: "Plane Rides," "Grocery Store Philosopher"

Something to note:

Admissions officers recognize that judging an essay is very subjective, and whether or not they admit your essay often comes down to something as simple as how much they like it, or the feeling they get from reading it. So, as obvious as it may sound, it is worth putting extra effort into making your essay interesting and likeable. Asking others (especially people older than you) to read your essay and provide feedback will help you do this.

We also want to add a warning though that this should come out completely naturally; forcing out quirkiness or trying too hard to be unique tends to backfire. Remember, *You* have a unique story to tell and our goal for this book is to help you unlock it. Every person is unique, so let that interesting story come out, instead of settling for gimmicks. This is a delicate balance; we hope that by reading the essays in this book, you can get a clear idea of what works and what doesn't, what is fun to read and what is cringe worthy. Always ask for an older person's opinion to make sure the unique, "personality" parts of your essay are not too weird, or that bits that are playful or funny are appropriate.

Says Something About Your Character and/or Motivations

This can't be emphasized enough. So much so, that it's worth repeating the old adage that The Admissions

Officers Are Really Reading This Essay To Learn More About You. The pieces that you can give the admissions officer that pertain to character, personality, drive, and motivation are the *most important, especially if they are written in a relatively interesting way.* Sometimes, students use an experience or a thought process to help demonstrate what makes them tick. An admissions officer wants to be able to imagine, as you walk across campus or as you participate in class, what kind of student you will be.

In fact, a phrase that can sometimes be heard flying around admissions committee tables is the Roommate Test — would this applicant make a good roommate? Colleges, of course, want good and kind people. This doesn't mean that you should try to explicitly show this in your essay; it's just something to keep in mind. Make sure the image you portray is congruent with these values.

Another thing to note is that Swarthmore Admissions is aligned with the faculty. Admissions has surveyed the faculty: "Over the years, who have you really loved to teach? What are the unique personality traits that would make a successful Swarthmore student?" As a result of this dialogue, intellectual curiosity and vibrancy is elevated at Swarthmore. **Swarthmore looks for intellectually curious students.** So it could be a good idea to mention that time you dug deep into an academic interest outside of class or explored new possibilities in your extracurriculars that took you to the next level.

Here's a list of qualities that the Swarthmore admissions team looks for in students. This can also be found on their website.

- **Intellectual curiosity and an enthusiasm for learning:** We are looking for students who genuinely enjoy learning and are uncommonly curious. Students relish the opportunities presented by our selection of 40+ academic programs, an extraordinarily devoted faculty, and a one-of-a-kind honors program.
- **Creative and proactive problem-solving:** We are intrigued by students who are flexible in their approach to learning, who are comfortable with experimentation, and who are willing to take intellectual risks that move them out of their comfort zone.
- **Generosity toward others:** We are looking for students who want to work with their peers, embrace collaboration, have a strong sense of empathy, and look for ways to support each other.
- **Civic engagement:** We appreciate students who have had a sustained commitment to service, who express a genuine interest in moving our world forward, and who demonstrate an interest in improving their school or local or cultural community in a collaborative way.
- **Willingness to work hard and to seek help:** The volume of commitments you will face at Swarthmore will demand a strong sense of organization. We are looking for students who have developed reliable work habits, an ability to focus on the task or commitment in front of them, and a willingness to use the support resources we provide.
- **Potential contributions to campus life:** Whether

you are from an urban center or a rural outpost (or somewhere in-between), we value your point of view. We are looking for students who will contribute their talents, interests, perspectives, and distinct voices to our community.

- **Sustained commitment:** We are more interested in your focus on a few activities over time (such as work, care for parents and siblings, service, or athletics), rather than membership in a long list of clubs—although we understand that some students can balance an assortment of activities.

- **Open-mindedness in general and to the liberal arts writ large:** Our most popular major tends to be "undecided," and we welcome everyone to the liberal arts tradition. We admit students to Swarthmore College, not a specific major. The ideal Swattie values humanities, the natural sciences and engineering, and the social sciences as lenses through which they can learn and grow.

Well-written

Many essay help books stress that the writing quality of the essay is not nearly as important as the content, i.e. that admissions officers care more about what you're saying than how you say it. However, at liberal arts colleges in particular, admissions officers care about how well you can write, because they want to know that you can handle the English classes that you will be required to take. They want to know that you can, in a sense, "do the liberal arts." That is not to say that your essay must have the most beautiful and eloquent writing, with SAT words riddled in every sentence. Absolutely not; in fact, we read quite a number of "admitted" essays that were

11

average in writing quality at best. (Remember, this essay is just *one part* of your application.) But, it is to say that there is some threshold when it comes to writing quality, and that liberal arts colleges like Swarthmore may care more about the writing quality and style than many other schools.

A couple of other qualifications: for mechanics and writing style, Swarthmore admissions adjusts expectations. An essay written by a student in a highly resourced environment where counselors spend hours helping students perfect their essays might be judged very differently than an essay written by a student from a school with hundreds of students per counselor.

How to Begin

Pick a question and a topic.

Starting is one of the hardest parts of the whole process. First, you'll have to pick a question to answer.

One good strategy is to look at the list of prompts and try to come up with ideas for each one. Hopefully, you'll be able to write up some initial brainstorms for each prompt. Some ideas will probably be easier to write about than others. From here, you can pick one or two ideas that are most interesting and true to you, and begin writing your essay!

Another strategy is to try to pinpoint the most interesting story you could possibly tell. A good brainstorming tactic for this is to sit down and write down as many meaningful experiences from your life as you can. Pick the one that is most engaging and provides the most fodder for reflection and showcasing your personality.

Lastly, if you're struggling a lot with figuring out what to write about, the following advice may be helpful. Good essay ideas often source from asking good questions. Here is a short list of questions we came up with to facilitate the brainstorming process:

Think about the significant moments in your life:
1. What are your greatest accomplishments/failures?
2. What is your most powerful childhood memory?
3. What are some of the challenges that you've faced? How did you respond?
4. What are some of the hardest choices you've had to make?

Think of your mentors, friends, and family:
1. How have your family and friends shaped who you are?
2. How did you choose your friends? What have they taught you?
3. Who are your role models? Why do you admire them?

We'd also advise looking up the article *How to Come Up With Great College Essay Ideas* on the PrepScholar website as well as the numerous posts from the The Koppelman Group for additional inspiration.

Don't stress too much about picking a topic that is extraordinary. Countless remarkable essays have been written about mundane, almost boring topics (example essay in this book: Grocery Store Philosopher). An example one admissions officer gave was an essay about the walls of a student's room. While it may sound like such an essay would be drier than, well, dry-wall, this author wrote about the music posters and diary postings he had hung up to elaborate on his interests and personality. What makes an interesting essay ultimately comes down to the voice, personality, and perspective you bring to it.

Write the essay

Once you've decided what you want to write about, it's time to put the pen to the paper. It is helpful sometimes to separate the "creative" and "revising" processes. Often, writers can get stuck in a loop of writing a few sentences and editing them endlessly. A helpful remedy that we have seen people use is writing all of their thoughts out, dumping everything they want to say onto the paper. Then, they go back and revise.

On the first draft, it is generally a good idea to ignore the word count and write everything you want to say. Then you can go back and cut out the unnecessary details, and refine it until it looks like a complete essay. Remember that most of the essays in this book have gone through countless drafts so don't be discouraged if your essay isn't quite up to **PAR** on your first try.

The PAR Framework

We want to introduce you to something we coined the PAR framework.

(P)ersonality, (A)ction, and (R)eflection: the three key components of an outstanding essay. Having one or two might give you something decent — there are plenty of great essays that only excel in the Personality and Reflection departments. But the best essays we've read are strong in all three. So let's go through each of them one by one.

Personality

Like we mentioned earlier, giving admissions officers a sense of who you are and what makes you tick is absolutely crucial. See the subsection titled "Interesting to Read" for some ways you can add personality into your essay.

Many applicants fall into the trap of thinking that the whole purpose of the application is to convince admissions officers that you are an accomplished person who will continue being accomplished in the future and bring prestige to Swarthmore's name. While this may be partially true, admissions officers also care a lot about building a class. What that means is that, for example, if the orchestra's timpani player just graduated, they may be keen on admitting timpani players this year. Or, if a lot of English Literature majors applied this year in particular, it may be harder to enter Swarthmore as an English Literature major. The same can be said about geographic location (i.e., they want to admit students from many different backgrounds, which means your chances may be higher coming from Nebraska than from California).

This is not to say that you should apply as a Gender and Sexuality Studies or Film Studies Major simply because there are fewer people applying with those intended majors. By the time you are a senior, most aspects of your application will be too late to change, so it is no use to worry about things that are out of your control, like what state you are applying from. We simply want to shed some light on the perspective of admissions officers. The fact that they care about building a class means that they care about the story and personality that a student brings to campus, because it gives them more information about the mix of individuals they are admitting. They want to admit people with interesting stories and diverse backgrounds, and the more you can convey specific aspects about your personality and interests — extrovertedness, sense of humor, nerdiness, love for music/sports/etc. — the better.

These elements will color how essay readers will remember your essay. When discussing your application, they might even begin associating your name with certain labels — the Airplane Pilot girl, or the Singing guy from Louisiana. We instinctively did the same after reading hundreds of essays. You want to write a memorable story full of details and experiences that highlight whichever parts of your personality you'd like your readers to remember you for.

Writing something unique or interesting about yourself while not being inauthentic is a delicate balance. In these situations it might be most helpful for a close friend or mentor to read your essay and give you feedback on whether or not the essay seems true to you. Just remember that personalizing your essay with colorful details about yourself will help you stand out and be more memorable to your readers.

Action

We want to be clear here. Writing resume-like descriptions about your accomplishments in your essay that could go in your Work and Activities section is a waste of space. Your essay should not read like a resume, and admissions officers are *specifically* looking for the elements of your experiences that can't quite be fully captured in the Work and Activities section, like how your experiences contributed to your personal growth. Out of the three components in PAR, this is probably the least essential.

However, it is also really important that your essay includes some degree of action and initiative. Talk is cheap. A very well-known and basic writing rule you want to follow is "Show, Not Tell." As much as you can, steer away from making baseless claims about yourself. Instead, write about an experience or tell a story about yourself that demonstrates those claims instead. After all, telling people that you're interested in computer science is a lot less convincing than showing off an app or website that you created. If you want to convey to your reader that you are persistent and self-motivated, include how you cooked breakfast and dinner for your family every day on top of homework and involvement in sports. Or, if you want to demonstrate that you are intellectually curious, write about how you used to spend hours watching Jeopardy and reading Wikipedia articles on Occam's Razor or Pascal's Wager, and how that eventually developed into a love for Quiz Bowl. Whatever it is, your actions can convey that you take initiative and demonstrate that you're a self-starter that will create real impact in the world.

We want to reiterate again, though, that this is not an absolute must-have for a great essay. Many terrific essays don't incorporate achievements or "concrete actions" at all, and you'll find a few examples of these in this book. Just keep in mind that it can help impress the reader if you weave in some of the things you've accomplished (i.e. simply mentioning them without describing them in detail) to help the reader envision you as a "doer" who can Make Things Happen, at Swarthmore and beyond.

At the end of the day, it's worth incorporating a sense of what you've accomplished in the essay. Make sure not to repeat any details you've included elsewhere in your application, and avoid describing your achievements in too much detail. Just think about mentioning them where they are related to your story. It can add substance behind your words.

Reflection

This is arguably the most neglected and most important part of the personal statement. It is absolutely crucial to have *at least some* reflection. While there are great essays in which the author did not include anything about their achievements, you will be hard-pressed to find an essay in this book that does not have any reflection. It is also perhaps the most difficult part to truly excel in. We can't tell you how many essays we read that had a great story but ended with weak reflection. This is where you can really stand out.

What do we mean by reflection? You can think of reflection as the "so-what?" — why were the experiences you are writing about important? What did you learn from them, how did they change or influence you, and how did you grow from them? Reflection can also be the parts of the essay that show your thought processes and self-awareness. Read "Plane Rides" and notice how the last paragraph dives deep into what debate means to the student and what role it has played in their life. For another example, read "The American Daydream" and "Better or Worse," where the author reflects on their "embryonic vision for their future." "Dancing Through Time" and "More Than Outcomes" are also great examples.

We want to refrain from writing too much about how to write good reflection because there isn't really a formula for how to do this. That's part of the reason why writing reflection is so hard. But, you can recognize good reflection when you see it, and we hope you can learn by example. This is one of the areas in which we hope this book can help the most.

Ultimately, reflection is conveying an awareness of who you are and the motivations behind the things you do. It covers the totality of your experiences while bringing to light the nuances of your thinking. Great reflection is insightful, above all other things. This is where you should write about something profound that you realized— about yourself, about your topic or experience, or about a lesson you learned. If you are stuck and can't come up with anything meaningful, a great place to look for ideas is conversations with friends and mentors. Have them ask you some deep questions to stir up some ideas. You can also read self help books to find some life lessons you may have learned from your experiences, and see how those lessons can be articulated.

We also want to emphasize the importance of having enough reflection to begin with. Many of the essays we read had great experiences, but only had a few sentences of reflection. For a loose estimate of how much is enough, 20-30% of the essay is a good benchmark. This is just a general rule of thumb to give you some idea of how much reflection to include. The reflection does not all have to be in one paragraph, and can be scattered throughout the essay. Remember that generating great reflection requires time, effort, and deep thought. It is not an easy thing to do, so don't fret too much if it doesn't come to you quickly. It isn't meant to. Sometimes, reflection just comes out naturally as you wrestle with your essay and think more about your story and its themes.

At all costs, avoid reflection that is superficial. A classic example of this is someone who travels to an impoverished area and sees that people there are actually "happy." Or a sports essay where the author failed and then worked hard to achieve their goals. There isn't much room for deep reflection here, and an admissions officer will roll their eyes from boredom.

Reflection is incredibly important, because it is where you get to show that you are thoughtful, and that you can clearly write about something you've learned. Colleges want to admit thoughtful, driven, and intellectually curious students, and the prime location to display this is in a reflective personal statement. Hopefully, the essays in this book will spark some ideas, and show you what good, insightful reflection looks like.

Common Essay Mistakes and Things to Avoid

    1. Not Talking About Yourself

Many students decide to write about someone influential in their life, whether it's their parents, grandparents, or mentors. While there is nothing inherently wrong about writing one of these essays, many students fall into the trap of writing their entire essay about that other person. Admissions officers might end up learning a lot about your mom or dad, but they'll be left wishing they knew more about you. Remember that admissions is not trying to admit your mom or grandpa. This mistake can also happen when your writing centers around a particular event with a nice story that never really reveals anything about yourself. Don't be a background character in your story. For every sentence that you include, you should ask yourself, what are you trying to show about yourself?

2. Including sentences that convey a judgmental or unpleasant attitude

There isn't much to say here, other than to be careful. Make sure to have at least a few people that you trust read your essay, so that they can help catch anything that might be misinterpreted. Also, it is a good idea to try to be as politically correct as possible. People of many different backgrounds — ethnicities, sexualities, genders, and ages — will be reading your essay.

3. Trying to write a sob story, or something that will invoke pity from the admissions officer

Generally, the advice we have heard here is to avoid writing about any topic that will still make you wince or feel discomfort when thinking about it. Admissions officers have made it very clear that they absolutely do not want students to write about anything that will bring them pain or cause them to relive trauma when writing this essay. Creating the personal statement should be fun and introspective, not harmful.

Note: Don't get too hung up on silly mistakes. Admissions officers will be understanding about grammar mistakes, so don't drive yourself crazy if you're not 100% sure whether or not a certain phrase is grammatically correct (although, of course, do strive to have correct grammar).

How Important is the Personal Statement?

Conventional college-app-writing wisdom says that the Personal Statement matters more for people who are "borderline." That is, it doesn't matter as much for students whose other components of the application (extracurriculars, test scores, grades, and recommendations) are very poor or very strong. It matters more for a student who is not a definite "yes" or definite "no."

However, Swarthmore loves to say that they evaluate students holistically, and in typical liberal arts fashion, care about "the whole person." Thus, they may weigh the essay a little more heavily than other schools, especially large schools that place more emphasis on test scores and GPA.

A fantastic personal statement can and has made admissions officers advocate for students to be accepted. An essay that connects really deeply with one admissions officer can spur them to advocate for your acceptance. That said, an amazing essay by itself will never single-handedly get you into Swarthmore. An application with a great essay usually gets admitted because the essay simply echoes how great the rest of the application is. Admissions decisions rarely hinge on an essay alone.

The Why Swarthmore Essay

This is your love letter to Swarthmore. It should answer questions like: Why are you and Swarthmore perfect for each other? Why are you in love with Swarthmore? What can you and Swarthmore gain from each other?

Writing this essay should be fairly formulaic. A great Why Swat essay does the following three things:

1. Writes about what you hope to take advantage of at Swarthmore, including very specific details unique to the college that show you've done your research.
2. Includes details from your past experiences to back this up.
3. Gives readers the sense that you will be a great personality/behavioral fit for Swarthmore

An admissions officer wants to avoid at all costs admitting someone who would hate being at Swarthmore and not contribute to the community at all. They are much more confident that you and Swarthmore will truly enjoy each other if you show that you've put in the time and effort to research Swarthmore. It will show that you truly know what Swarthmore is all about, that you have some idea of what being there would be like, and that you liked what you saw enough to actually apply with a well-written essay. It will demonstrate that you aren't just applying to get into an elite college, and that you don't just "feel like" you would like it. To do that, you want to show that there are specific things — concrete reasons — unique to Swarthmore that you really love.

One great way of doing this is to find and talk about quintessential Swarthmore traditions. Good examples include Pterodactyl Hunt, Ninjagrams, Screw your Roommate, and the Crum Regatta.

See the "Tour of Swarthmore" chapter. The whole purpose of that chapter is to help you write those Swarthmore-specific things for your Why Swarthmore essay! **Pick three or four things that really speak to you and write about why you love them so much.**

Include Details From Your Past Experiences

Your reasons for wanting to go to Swarthmore will only be compelling if you have the track record to prove that you'll do the things you say you'll do and that you're interested in the things you say you're interested in. It'll demonstrate authenticity and give you more room to show off your accomplishments, thought processes, and personality!

Example: You want to join A Capella group at Swat? Preface that by talking about your 3 years of experience in high school A Capella, choir, or Glee Club. Then write about how you hope to *continue* pursuing this passion of yours at Swarthmore. That's a lot more believable and convincing than "it has always been my dream to be a great singer."

Give the Reader the Sense that Your Personality is a Match for

Swarthmore

This isn't absolutely necessary, but it is helpful if the reader can easily imagine you at Swarthmore. If you've done the previous two pieces of advice well, this should hopefully already be in place. But some indicators that will signal to admissions officers that you are a good fit for Swarthmore include a love for learning for the sake of learning (e.g. being nerdy/intellectual) and having diverse interests. As evidenced by the list of traits that they look for in Swarthmore students, admissions officers care a lot that you are open-minded. This means they want to make sure that you aren't the type of student that has a rigid plan to only take economics classes and go directly into finance. In other words, it is a good sign if you are demonstrating a "liberal arts" mindset. Our advice here is to avoid exhibiting a pre-professional or cutthroat bent. That's a red flag to admissions officers that you probably don't belong at a place like Swarthmore.

A mistake to avoid: Again, no need to fret too much over grammar mistakes. However, it will raise some eyebrows if your "Why Swat" essay repeatedly refers to Swarthmore as "Swarthmore University." A mistake like this conveys to the reader that you didn't really do your research, and it draws a question mark on whether or not you'd truly be a match for Swarthmore.

II. SWARTHMORE ADMISSIONS OFFICER Q&A

1. Can you give students an idea of what happens to their applications and essays after they are received by the college?

When a student applies to Swarthmore, a committee of admissions deans reviews the application. First, at least two deans sit down together, review all of the application components, including essay(s), and discuss the strengths of the applicant. We take into account what opportunities and resources the student has had access to, their high school's curriculum, their geographic location, their family background, and their cultural identity. If we believe a student might be a good fit for Swarthmore, the application will move past the first review to additional reviews and discussions. By the time we offer a student admission, the application may have been reviewed by as many as half a dozen committees, each of which considers the full context of a student's background, experiences, and opportunities.

There is no formula for admission to Swarthmore. We do not admit students based on a single factor or one person's opinion. Each admission decision is the result of a thorough, committee-based, holistic, contextual, and highly selective application evaluation.

2. What are the key things admissions officers look for in the personal statement? (And how might the Swarthmore Admissions evaluation process differ from other schools?)

High school students are often really good at describing an experience, activity, or person they admire, which is a good start. But we want to see a bit more analysis. We care more about *why* they engaged in an activity and how it impacted them versus what the activity is. What did they learn from being challenged in class, on the field, in a job, or at home while caring for siblings, and how have they grown as a result of the experience? Students will sometimes write about someone they admire, and by the end of the essay, we want to admit the person being described. The student may forget to share what they learned and who they have become from admiring this person, leaving us knowing very little about them. In essence, we want to see a bit more analysis and less description. The topic is less important than the potential we see as we compare the essay to other parts of the application. Is the student capable of writing at the college level? We do not want nor do we expect a perfect writing sample; rather, we want some evidence of intellectual depth and/or potential.

3. The Swarthmore Application gave three options for the supplemental essay this year. Can you explain why that changed and what you're looking for in these supplemental essays?

For decades, we have asked students, in a supplemental essay, why they have chosen to apply to Swarthmore College. We have also worked hard to provide access to diverse groups of students, and we continually look for more opportunities to do so. During the current pandemic, we moved to a two-year, test-optional policy. Given the importance of essays in the process, we decided to add a few more options to choose from, understanding that most if not all prospective students will not have had a chance to visit campus in person. By adding these essay choices, we believe students will be able to find one supplemental question they are comfortable answering. We also wanted to give students a chance to share how their community has impacted them or share with us an example of intellectual risk-taking, while still leaving them the option to tell us, why Swarthmore? Offering a few more choices seemed right, particularly now.

4. How important is the personal statement? The supplemental?

Personal statements and supplemental essays round out the application and give students a chance to personally share with the admissions committee what they feel is most important to them at this juncture in their burgeoning academic, social, and intellectual journey. Essays in particular may play a different role depending on the student and their background and experiences. Because we read holistically — meaning we look at many factors when reviewing an application — even a stellar essay is unlikely to outweigh a poor academic performance or a lack of rigorous preparation, while a compelling application might be tipped into the class by a particularly strong essay. The importance of the writing truly depends on the individual and the context.

5. What are some of the most common mistakes that students make on the personal statement and on the supplemental? Are there topics students should avoid, and if so, what are they? For the Why Swat Essay, are there reasons that you're tired of hearing, e.g. the honors program or the 8:1 teacher to student ratio? What are some red flags?

Often, students do not proofread their essays, and many students wait until the last minute to complete them. Like any essay or written project for high school, one should not submit the first draft as the final draft. College essays — personal statements and supplementals — take work, some forethought, and revision. Some students tend to regurgitate what they find on the website, but we want to know why they have applied to Swarthmore specifically. Mentioning that we are a small, highly selective residential liberal arts college describes many of our closest peers, but that does not show us that a student has researched our mission, offerings, what they might gain from being on our campus, and how they might grow and develop here. Our size and location may be an advantage, but why? Does it impact students that Swarthmore offers engineering in a liberal arts context? What is different about our Honors program versus traditional university Honors Colleges? Why might a student pursue that option once on campus? Many essays describe the liberal arts in general but not Swarthmore, and we do believe we are distinctive from our peers. If a student has only a general impression about Swarthmore, then they might want to answer one of the other questions or choose to do a little bit of homework on why they might take the time to complete our application. With a little forethought and planning, we know students will produce solid and compelling essays for college admission. We wish students all the best in the process and with their college search!

III. YOUR WRITTEN TOUR OF SWARTHMORE

Knowing Swarthmore well will help you write a terrific *Why Swarthmore* essay and help you decide if Swat is the right school for you! If you aren't able to visit Swarthmore, don't worry. We've compiled all the information you'd receive if you went on a campus tour based on our conversations with several Swarthmore (Swattie) student tour guides.

Academics

This will make up the bulk of your experience at Swarthmore. The first semester for all incoming freshmen is pass-fail at Swarthmore, meaning that none of your grades from the classes you take your first semester will appear on your transcript (although you will still receive "shadow grades," so you know what grades you would have gotten). This policy is meant to help freshmen as they make the transition to college-level work and encourage them to explore subject areas that they might not be as familiar with without worrying that it might negatively impact their GPA. You also get four pass-fail classes you can take throughout your four years at Swarthmore. Bombed a midterm? Feel free to pass-fail that class. If you end up doing well, you always have the option to uncover your grade.

If you need help with certain concepts or guidance on your homework, there are plenty of peer tutoring resources for students. Programs like Pi-rates (Math), Wizards (Engineering), Ninjas (Computer Science), Alchemists (Chemistry), and The Visible Hands (Economics) all are present to assist you. These tutoring resources are run by students who are required to sit in on all the lectures that you're in. That way they know what material you're currently learning as well as the teaching style of your professor. At Swarthmore, classes are never taught by teacher's assistants; they are always taught by professors, although sometimes students who've already taken the course may be present to give one on one help within larger lectures. However, most class sizes are small enough (the average being fourteen students) that it's easy to ask questions in class, after class, or during office hours. You frequently run into professors on campus and it's easy to build close relationships with them. Swatties are for the most part collaborative, and competition between students is close to non-existent.

Academics are also closely tied with social justice at Swarthmore. Countless classes engage with the community and are designed to encourage students to think about ways they can positively impact others. Examples include courses like the Sociology of Education where students are encouraged to apply their knowledge to developing policies and practices for schools from the PreK-12 level.

At Swat, interdisciplinary studies are required

through the distribution requirements that mandate students take courses in the humanities, social sciences, and natural sciences. Almost no one at Swarthmore has just one major and double majors and minors are common. People's majors also don't always "make sense," and students have been known to major in fields as unrelated as cognitive science and theater, math and studio art, etc.

One of Swarthmore's unique aspects is their honors program. Students have to wait until the end of their sophomore year to declare their majors. There are no caps on the number of students accepted into a major and even after declaring a major sophomore year you can still shift your areas of study or add minors. Sophomore year is also when you can choose whether or not to take the honors track for your major (pending approval from departmental advisors). Honors is not a separate college within Swarthmore and it isn't necessarily even what the "smartest" students do. It is simply an option for people who want to explore a particular subject deeply. The two-credit seminars that students take, involving heavy amounts of reading and in-class discussions, are a central feature of the honors program. At the end of senior year, Swarthmore invites examiners, who are experts in their fields, from different institutions to come and evaluate honors students to decide if they should graduate with honors, and if so, whether they should obtain the distinctions of honors, high honors, or highest honors. These outside examiners have sole responsibility for these decisions and base their evaluations on students' performances in written and oral exams that they administer. Seniors regularly say that meeting with the external examiners is the most exciting (and stressful!)

part of the honors program. Sometimes, you even get to meet an examiner whose research you've read and cited in your work. If you're feeling courageous, you might even tell them what you disagreed with in their research and propose some of your ideas.

There are three main libraries at Swarthmore: McCabe (Humanities and Social Sciences), Cornell (STEM), and Underhill (Music and Dance). Students can go to any of the libraries but each only holds books and other materials in their respective subject area. Each library has quiet areas (and sometimes floors) for those that like to work in silence as well as more social spots. They also have conference rooms where you can hold meetings with your classmates. Swarthmore librarians are great at helping students with their research essays and assignments, whether that means looking for sources or how to best structure your paper. They are extremely knowledgeable and will save you a lot of time!

Swarthmore is also part of the Tri-College Consortium, composed of Swarthmore, Bryn Mawr, and Haverford. This means that Swarthmore students can take classes at Bryn Mawr and Haverford and that there are regular shuttles that go between the schools. Also, as part of the Quaker Consortium, Swatties can take courses at the University of Pennsylvania. Haverford and Bryn Mawr are very close schools, and 90% of Haverford students will take a class at Bryn Mawr, and vice versa. By contrast, the percentage of Haverford and Bryn Mawr students who take classes at Swarthmore is in the single digits. Some tour guides like to say that we are the very nerdy cousin that lives across the city. You're not going to see Bryn Mawr or Haverford regularly unless you make the effort. Meanwhile, Penn is the rich uncle upstate that you need to take the train to reach. Many students frequently visit University City (a part of Philly that essentially houses UPenn and Drexel) to see friends. University City also has great restaurants.

Extracurriculars

With over 100 clubs at Swarthmore, there are lots of things to get involved in. From pre-professional clubs like 180 Degrees Consulting (Management Consulting) and Clarus Capital (Finance) to acapella groups (5 in total) to mock trial and cultural clubs, there is sure to be something that matches your interests. Check the Swarthmore website for a complete list of clubs and activities. If you want to start something on campus that isn't already there, the school is supportive and generous with its funding for new clubs. Students have even created a pyro club where they set random objects on fire! Pretty much whatever activity you want (as long as it's legal, of course) can become a club and receive funding at Swarthmore.

Recreational sports like soccer, tennis, water polo, frisbee, and rugby all have teams on campus, and many students participate. Swarthmore also has events like SwatTank (our version of Shark Tank) where students are encouraged to pitch their business ideas.

Swarthmore is an NCAA Division Three school and competes in the Centennial Conference. A sizable number of students are also athletes and can successfully balance schoolwork, clubs, and sports. Coaches understand that academics come first and the *student* in student-athlete is emphasized. While athletes never miss class for practice, occasionally classes will be skipped for games when athletes aren't able to choose a class schedule that doesn't conflict with games.

A side note that has to do with extracurriculars, but also ties into many other aspects of campus life, is that Swarthmore is a cash-free campus. This means that all student activities are paid for by the "activities fees" portion of your tuition. Because of this, clubs don't have registration fees and travel costs for events or tournaments are covered. Amenities like laundry and printing are also all free and food on campus can be bought by swiping your student ID.

Housing and Food

Most students live on campus all four years at Swarthmore. Freshman are randomly assigned roomates but sophomores can choose who they room with. Typically juniors and seniors get singles. Having a fan in your room is a must as most dorms don't have air conditioning and it can get hot at certain times of the year.

Swarthmore has one main dining hall (Sharples), a snack bar/grill (Essie Mae's), and two coffee bars (Science Center/Kohlberg). Sharples is completely free of nut based products and has a gluten free and vegetarian section as well. Although students often like to complain about the food, it is edible and sometimes quite tasty. When all else fails, pizza and burgers are always an option. Students can also choose meal plans with fewer Sharples meal swipes and more "points," which they can spend at Science Center and Kohlberg. Both usually have catered meals from Asian restaurants for Lunch that are quite good.

Traditions

Swat can get weird. Like real weird. Here are some (but not all!) of the traditions that happen each year on campus:

- Primal Scream - During the last week of reading period before finals, students gather at Sharples (the dining hall) and eat a late-night breakfast served by the staff. When midnight strikes, students scream as loud as they can, releasing all of their stress and anxiety! It didn't work for us but we did enjoy the midnight waffles....
- Pterodactyl Hunt - Coordinated every year by the members of the Psi Phi Club, the Pterodactyl hunt is a live action battle to the death event that takes place all across campus.
- Screw Your Roommate - No, it's not what you think it is. Every Valentine's Day, friends match each other with dates and have them dress up in themed costumes. Students then gather in Sharples to find their date who is wearing a complimentary costume. Some past pairs include Doctor and pepper, dog and fire hydrant, and supply and demand curves.
- Ninja Grams - Every St. Valentine's day, an army of Ninjas emerge to deliver Valentine's Day cards to their targets. Whether you're in class, the dining hall, or just walking about the ninjas will accomplish their mission!
- Crum Regatta - Each spring during parents weekend, Swatties rush to build a wide variety of boats and rafts to race down the Crum Creek. Look on You-

Tube for a wild video to see the event in action.

- Winter Formal - Usually in January, students get fancy for this event. With a live DJ, food, and games, this is one of the largest parties of the year.

Research, Internships, and Post-Grad Outcomes

Because Swarthmore is an undergraduate only institution, there are many opportunities for students to get involved with research. In fact, two-thirds of Swarthmore students do research with a faculty member at some point in their Swarthmore career. Usually, faculty will post research positions they have available or students will reach out to professors they are interested in to see if they require any help. For students who participate in summer research, the Lang Center provides grants and will pay students to do ten weeks of research during that time. The Lang Center also has grants for students who do unpaid internships during the summer that align with social justice and any of the Lang Center initiatives.

Students apply for internships through an online platform called Handshake. Career Services is extremely accessible and provides resume and cover letter reviews while also giving guidance on how to explore potential careers. They even have a "library of suits" where students can borrow suits for job interviews and recruiting events! They don't want something like formal work attire to prevent you from obtaining job opportunities. A popular program offered at Swarthmore is the Swarthmore Future Entrepreneurs Program (SFEP) where students are paired with startups near Swarthmore and provided funding to work there during the summer. Career services also offers externships, which are week long job shadows with Swarthmore alumni that usually occur the last week of winter break. Students are able to see what it's like to work in careers ranging from being an attorney at the Department of Justice to working as a software engineer at a tech startup.

70% of Swarthmore graduates end up going to grad school within five years of graduation, and many go on to earn PhDs. Swarthmore has extremely good placement into top graduate programs and this is one of the main strengths of Swarthmore. However, it's important to note that Swarthmore is not a top target school for consulting and finance. Some consulting and finance firms do recruit actively at Swat, like BCG, Treacy, Citi, and T. Rowe Price. However, for most firms, networking is very important for landing interviews. There is a benefit to going to a school like Swat, whose primary focus isn't career-oriented, which is that it is much easier to be a big fish in a small pond. Swat alumni go out of their way to help Swatties, and will not hesitate to dump resources on you. Ultimately, if you are interested in consulting or finance at Swarthmore and you put in the work by networking and practicing for interviews, getting a job in consulting or finance should be no problem.

The same can be said for tech. For tech, the recruiting process does not change too much in difficulty from school to school. Of course, there are some schools that receive special treatment, like MIT or Berkeley, but ultimately your chances of getting into a FAANG company at Swarthmore does not differ drastically from your chances at UPenn, Columbia, or other elite institutions.

Surrounding Environment

Swarthmore's campus is gorgeous. The Scott Arboretum is part of the campus and students are often awestruck by the greenery and flowers as soon as they step foot on campus. The famous Magill walk that extends from Parrish Hall to the train station is beautiful to stroll down and you get to see a different side of it as the seasons change. If you're looking to get into nature to destress, the Crum Woods extend out west of the main campus and is a great place to go for a short hike. The outdoor amphitheater where graduation occurs is one of a kind, truly cementing the end of your four years at Swat where you've made memories that will last a lifetime. One thing is for sure: you won't be graduating in some crowded football stadium!

The local area is a typical quiet, suburban neighborhood, and the Ville is a small downtown area right off of Swarthmore's campus. Admittedly, there isn't much there. There are a few barbershops, a Dunkin Donuts, breakfast restaurants, a grocery store, and an Asian restaurant. If you're looking for a vibrant city life right *at* your college campus, you will not get that at Swarthmore. What Swarthmore conveniently does have is a train that runs right through the edge of campus, which students who are craving more excitement can take to go into Philadelphia. The SEPTA ticket lotteries that Swarthmore holds are a great way to go on a free trip to the city with friends. Many students are able to fit weekly or monthly visits into Philadelphia into their schedule, but there are also lots of students who expect to do this and never end up doing it because they are too busy with Swarthmore academics and activities. It is a thirty-minute train ride to the city center. Swarthmore also provides weekly shuttles to a local Target, the King of Prussia Mall, and movie theatres. So whether you need to buy more detergent or catch the latest action movie, Swat's got you covered. For short trips, Media, the local town nearby, is a popular destination to go out and get food (since it's only ten minutes away) and is a good option if you don't want to go into Philly.

Culture

Swarthmore has a very distinct personality and culture that permeates throughout the student body. By and large, students are extremely conscious of BIPOC and LGBTQ+ issues and tend to be more progressive. Students aren't afraid to call out perceived injustices and oppression. The strong social justice conscience is reflected in the many clubs, courses, and opportunities emphasizing activism and action for social issues.

Swarthmore is also small which contributes to the tight-knit feel of the student body. You frequently run into the same people in class, in the dining hall, and around campus. By the time you're a senior, you'll know most of your class (or at the very least recognize their faces), and hopefully have built close relationships with many of them.

Swatties also take school and homework extremely seriously. At Swat, saying you have an essay to work on as an excuse to not go hang out is a valid excuse. People respect work and making work-life priorities. On the flip side, because Swatties are so driven, sometimes they can get burnt out by involving themselves in too many things on top of their rigorous academics. Luckily, Swatties are always supportive and the academic environment is collaborative with little to no competition. There are always study groups going on and people wanting to help each other out. Swatties tend to be extremely passionate and diverse in their interests. This makes for interesting classroom discussions and exposes students to a wide variety of viewpoints and opinions.

Real Talk

Swarthmore is not perfect and neither is any other school. However, Swarthmore can be a terrific place to spend four years as long as you earnestly evaluate whether or not you would fit in there— independent of whatever the college rankings say. We can't tell you if Swarthmore is right for you nor can anyone else. But we do think that getting as much information as possible will go a long way towards helping you make an informed decision (and help you write a better essay), and we strongly advise you to reach out to current Swarthmore students and alumni to get a more accurate picture of what it's like there. Swatties are always willing to help and we guarantee that you will learn a lot through even a fifteen-minute phone call with one of them. Swarthmore admissions have a great resource called "Ask a Swattie" where you can email students and get their perspective on Swarthmore. Simply search it up online, email a Swattie, and schedule a call with one of them!

IV. THE ESSAYS

COMMON APPLICATION ESSAYS

To Punch the Way of the Teacher
Skylar Thoma

"How good are you in a fight?" I'm often asked, when people find out I practice martial arts. I answer automatically, usually saying "pretty good." But that question always leads me to one of my guru's key sayings: "Throughout history, those who loved to fight were destroyed, but those who did not know how to fight were also destroyed. Strength and virtue -- only those together can lead others." The emphasis on virtue cannot be appreciated until after strength is pushed to the limit.

I practice Poekoelan Tjiminde Tulen (or Poekoelan, for "short"), which originates from Indonesia and emphasizes self-defense, animal movements, dynamic forms, and free sparring. I started in first grade, and loved it despite the challenges. However, no challenge compared to my test for brown sash in 2012. During a 24-hour period, wannabe brown sashes must remain awake and ready, run five miles and demonstrate all they have learned over their years of training. What's more, I was given no advance warning; my guru decided I was ready, and I had to -- literally -- hit the ground running. When I emerged after the craziest 24 hours of my life, I felt like I was at the top of the world, having attained the rank just below black belt. I didn't realize at the time, however, that a new direction in my training had begun.

I assumed I would continue to focus on learning forms and self-defense techniques. Instead, most of my time at the studio now revolves around personal development and teaching others. Brown sash represents the roots of Poekoelan, a commitment to fully understanding the art and teaching the students who are following in your footsteps. So I began to run warm-ups, dictate cleaning responsibilities after class, and teach lower-ranking students the techniques I had been taught many years ago. This, however, wasn't as easy as I thought it was going to be. The first time I ran a warm-up session, I was too hesitant and vague with my instructions. The higher-ranking instructors "gently" helped me along by pressing me for the next instruction, or providing it if necessary. My initial rocky experiences teaching in the studio washed away my ego, replacing it with a desire to improve. This time, however, I wanted to improve as a teacher, not as a student.

"With great power comes great responsibility" is perhaps the most overused quote in comic book cinema. However, Spiderman's Uncle Ben neglected to make this addendum: with great responsibility comes great humility. Before I became brown sash, my goals were self-centered. I was always fretting over my ability to break a board, or perform leaping kicks, or do fancy kip-ups. After attaining brown sash, those concerns became secondary, behind my shortcomings as a leader and teacher. Eventually, I became more self-confident and articulate, filling in my role as a leader in the school community.

When rehearsing for a tournament last September, my job was to prepare the kids' self-defense demonstrations. One student, a shy third-grader named Miriam, was breaking down with nervousness and frustration at the first practice. I did my best to console her and give her positive feedback, and she gradually became more confident and assertive. At the tournament, I won second place in forms, but I spent most of my time cheering my teammates and watching Miriam win the self-defense category with flying colors.

At the end of every Poekoelan class, each student shakes the hand of everyone in the room, no matter the age or rank, and says "gotong royong," which loosely translates to "I learn from you, and you learn from me." Since testing for brown sash, I've learned just how true that statement is. "Gotong royong" represents the rewards of contributing to the community: self-confidence, communication skills, and gratitude. I am now more prepared and more eager to contribute in college, in work, in family, and beyond.

Analysis

This essay is a great piece on community and giving back. We see true leadership and the growth that comes from mentorship and cultivating the best in others. The essay is not particularly flowery but is an honest and well-thought-out piece of writing. The closing paragraph and it's inclusion of the phrase "Gotong royong" encapsulates the ideals within the essay and is a pleasant conclusion.

The author demonstrates a love for an obscure and fascinating subject (something common to many Swarthmore students), which is perhaps especially appealing to colleges like Swarthmore. It is sprinkled with interesting adages, and it isn't predictable. Because of these elements, it is interesting to read, and shows a high level of intellectual vibrancy. Moreover, the writer's voice shows through in a strong way, with well-structured and clearly written thinking.

The author's story writing skills are also superb. They are a dynamic character in their own story, meaning that their character has undergone a significant inner change between the beginning and the end. They go from being a timid, slightly awkward, more self-oriented person to, in their words, a more self-confident and articulate leader. The reader is able to see then mature into a dependable and responsible mentor who can emotionally support an anxious pupil during a nervous breakdown. This sense of transformation is extremely important for telling a good story. Certain types of essays require there to be a clear change, whether that is a shift in mindset or a lesson learned, between who the author is at the beginning and who they are at the end of the story. Generally, for this type of essay, a person reading your personal statement should be able to quickly identify what that change is. If your essay has a story like this one, make sure your essay answers the question: how have you grown through the experiences in your essay? What have you learned?

Another great aspect of this writer's story-writing skills pertains to the amount of specific detail in this story. Their descriptions are of concrete actions, and you can imagine them as they run their five miles for their test, or as they teach their students the techniques they have learned. They are specific. Instead of saying that their mentors helped them learn how to be an assertive leader, they *show* this by mentioning that his instructors pressed them for the next instruction when they were too hesitant. They are not vague or general. They state that their goals were previously self-centered, but they then elaborate on how they had focused more on how to "break a board, or perform leaping kicks, or do fancy kip-ups" in the past. These details also help readers visualize the sport. "Show, Not Tell" is the name of the game.

You also get the sense that no words are wasted in this essay. Every sentence contributes to painting a picture of his journey and his character development. In this essay, the author has managed to fit in a though-provoking intro, a grueling test that captures "the craziest 24 hours" of his life, his growth into an effective teacher, a specific experience demonstrating the culmination of that growth (helping Miriam), and a great meditation on "gotong royong" in his experiences to wrap it all up. Imitate this efficient yet descriptive storytelling by avoiding spending words on things that don't tell the reader anything about you.

Melanin Meadow
Shannon Billups

I once read a book where the author referenced Junot Díaz who said, "If you want to make a human being into a monster, deny them, at the cultural level, any reflection of themselves." That quote had a profound impact on how I started to think about racial identity. It wasn't the thoughtfulness of the statement that impacted me. It was the terrifying implications of the statement that suggests the ability to be turned into something negative if you don't see yourself reflected in what is good, or what is high achieving, or what has some power. The same idea comes up again in a Kendrick Lamar song, *The Blacker the Berry*. At the end of the song, Lamar says the words, "So why did I weep when Trayvon Martin was in the street, when gang banging make me kill a n***a blacker than me? Hypocrite!" He explains why this happens throughout the whole song, how warped perceptions of entire groups of people can be detrimental to one's sense of self and could ultimately create a "monster".

As someone that grew up in a predominantly white and working class community, I know what it's like to not see yourself reflected positively on the screens or in books. I also know what it's like to not see yourself reflected positively in daily life since terms like achievement gap and sub group are directed at minority students in school. Fellow classmates had bought into stereotypes of what it means to be black and I always felt that they saw me as more of an exception to an unwritten rule. So, when my sister called me with an idea to start a website so that black girls like us would be able to see themselves as the amazing people they are, I was all for it. Melanin Meadow is a website my sister and I created that can be used as not only a resource where people can see positive images of black women, but also as a way for black girls to interact and share ideas, submit art and writing, and to recognize the beauty in themselves.

Everyone should be able to see positive reflections of themselves in everyday life. That's what we strive to show black girls through Melanin Meadow. We show them that they can be scientists, they can be doctors, they can be writers and actors and artists. *I* get to see that I can be all of those things through all of the research I do. I get to see all of the books, movies, and television shows written by and starring black women. I get to see various famous black women in science, technology, engineering, mathematics and politics. I get to read about the stories of black women like Shirley Chisholm and Maya Angelou and learn about all the famous events in black women's history. Most importantly, I get to know that other black girls get to learn about those things as well.

Working on this website with my sister is a meaningful experience that I will continue as I expand and grow during my college years. The knowledge that I've gathered and the sense of self that I am slowly discovering are two things that I hope to continue to develop in a space where differences are celebrated and valued. I also want to give back to a community of learners that includes girls like me. Even if there's only one girl that is able to see themselves reflected back to them positively through Melanin Meadow, I will know that I am halting the creation of more monsters.

Analysis

The author begins with a superb analysis of two very different types of writers. This immediately plunges the reader into the writer's reflections and ideas. It also introduces the reader to the types of content this writer loves to consume by quoting both a Pulitzer Prize winning MIT creative writing professor and a pop culture figure who is widely acknowledged as the greatest rapper of all time. You can tell a lot about this person just by reading their intro.

This essay also tackles a difficult topic: racism. A common pitfall for this type of essay is to let it spiral into a vague condemnation of racial injustice. However, this student keeps their essay personal and relatable by tying the themes of racism and prejudice into their own life and their own deep-seated desire to see women of color succeed. The author shows their personal journey to creating their website, "Melanin Meadow," and through it, we are able to see this student's thoughtfulness, heart, and maturity.

Plane Rides
Megan Wu

For most debaters, the narrative of competing at tournaments is simple: drive to the airport with your team the day before rounds start, board a plane to your destination, and stay in a nice-enough hotel with a nightly room check and multiple chaperones, all done on the school's dime.

The same is not true for me: I've flown to eighteen tournaments alone over the past two years. Though I can't afford to bring an adult to ensure my safety at every moment, I compete anyways. The national circuit gives me the opportunity to debate complex and meaningful issues that I can't anywhere else—hence, my two-year long adventure as a lone-wolf debater.

Surprisingly, my best strategies in debate rounds are often produced through the unique combination of navigating across the country by myself and walking into rounds without enough prep because I'd had IB assessments due the week of the tournament. Judges often tell me that my desperate, last-ditch strategic evasions in round (or—as I later describe them to my coach—inventive tactical calls) are creative and innovative. My gambits are most often generated from permuting my opponent's mistakes and the arguments I do have. In that sense, debating with fewer resources at my disposal challenges me to make novel connections between the hidden similarities of different arguments. But the usefulness of learning to strategically pivot in a split-second is most visible when my travel plans go awry—from helping a woman who only spoke Spanish navigate a closed subway stop in the Bronx to calling a locksmith to inspect a locked Airbnb door, debate has taught me independence and how to thrive on my own.

Though the lone-wolf moniker may apply to me because I'm invariably the only one from my school at tournaments, I have rarely felt truly alone around other debaters. The abundant debate resources on blogs and Youtube have trained me. My friends on the national circuit have always been supportive and welcoming, inviting me to stay in their homes during tournament weekends. The understanding and acceptance I have felt over the years has made the barriers to competing on the national circuit challenges I can conquer, rather than insurmountable obstacles.

When I sit on planes heading north from LA, or Ubers driving through Minneapolis, or trains snaking their way through Connecticut, I often find myself wondering if spending the money and time to compete in this activity, far from my family and homework, is worth it. When I'm alone with only my thoughts and the drone of transportation humming in my ears, my answer to this question is sometimes colored with regret that I didn't win more rounds at that weekend's tournament or excitement to get back to school and my internship. But, after so many cities and rounds, I am intensely grateful for the way that debate has filled my life. It overflows out of the weekend tournaments: arguments in debate rounds are a distilled version of the philosophy I read at my internship, and an aff case about womens' education abroad is what inspired me to fundraise for menstrual health in developing countries. Over the years, debate has splashed onto my Tuesdays and Thursdays, when I teach my novices and middle schoolers, and has trickled into Wednesday afternoons spent preparing for that weekend's tournament.

I have been on one long plane ride over the past two years, and I have loved every second of it.

Analysis

This essay says a lot with few words. Details like "helping a woman who only spoke Spanish... calling a locksmith to inspect..." show us (show, not tell!) that this person is an independent and resilient problem-solver. The passion for debate is clear but perhaps even clearer is that the student's pursuit for knowledge and excellence aren't just limited to this activity— it impacts everything they do. Debate just happens to be the perfect medium for them to demonstrate their intelligence and creativity.

No Beard For Now
Haron Kalii

I am alone in my room; scared, ill at ease. I cannot seem to find a comfortable spot. The bed? No, that's too high. The floor? No, I won't be able to see my reflection. I pick a stool and a small table. On the table is a basin with water, my head is bent with my face close to the water. My palms are wet, beads of perspiration are forming on my nose, I have butterflies in my stomach, my hands are trembling, and then the razor falls out of my hand. This is the first time I am going to shave my small beard, and I don't know where to start. The Kwenzwa ceremony, the shaving of one's first beard, is typically a communal celebration in Kamba culture, but planning a village celebration means that I will be expected to get married in less than three months. So instead, I have to shave in the secrecy of my room.

My bodily discomfort recalls memories of when I first joined high school. A time when I could not communicate fluently in English without dropping in an accidental nini, a Swahili placeholder, exposing my linguistic struggle. I walked in silence looking for people with similar tribulations so that I could find comfort in their midst.

I have yet to draw the razor across my chin. I am staring at myself in my small handheld mirror. I am wondering if this man in the reflection has any suggestions on where to begin.

Having a beard, where I come from, means that I am now a man. It means that I can no longer live under my parents' roof. It means that my grandmother will start suggesting which girls in the village I should marry. It means that I will start receiving small notes detailing the cost of things I have to buy in the house. I am not ready for what is expected of me. I want to pursue my academic interests, rather than settle down to raise a family with a woman from the village. I want to venture beyond what my community expects of me. That is why I cannot let this beard grow any further. I've got to cut it down: defer my introduction into manhood.

Eventually, I get the grip on my razor right. I have summoned myself and concluded that I have no choice. The time to leave my beard untouched has not yet come, I cannot take that road.

Again, my awkwardness brings me back to high school, to another time when I had summoned myself and decided that I'd had enough. I could not walk speechless simply because my English was entangled in my heavy Kamba accent. I began working on my vocabulary and accent. The dictionary became a friend. I learned words and had my desk mate quiz me on their meaning. I joined the debate team and argued my points as much as I could, in English—even when debaters were free to use Swahili.

Shaving, on the other hand, is not going as smoothly. The furtive strategy has gone horribly wrong: I've cut myself. I am bleeding. I'd thought that at the end of it all I would break into a victory dance, but instead I have to hide evidence of my bloodied face. I do hope, in the near future, to master the skill.

I want to be free— free from the shackles of a tradition that denigrates the pursuit of education. In my quest to continue my education, I also hope to keep a well groomed beard on my chin without having to worry about what number of children will be whispered into my ear for me to beget. I will define my own appearance and my own future.

Analysis

In this powerful essay, readers can witness this student's genuine pursuit of education in the context of growth into manhood. The portion of the essay about this student's dedication to improving their English demonstrates their determination and drive. But perhaps most impressive is their finding the strength to carve out a non-conventional path despite community expectations. Although this essay's specific story may not apply to most students, writers should aim to emulate this essay's ability to showcase desired qualities like determination and independence and tell a unique story.

Food Is A Celebration of Our Blessings
Anonymous

"Every good chef must know how to properly cook an egg," my mother's voice sang from above as I stood on my tiptoes and peered at the gooey whites of an egg bubbling and blistering in the skillet. The summer I asked my mother to teach me to cook has undoubtedly altered the path of my life forever -- and it has certainly changed the lives of those who eat that which I prepare. Having been born and raised in Atlanta, Georgia, soul food is very important to my southern heart. In the tiny kitchen of our beach condo in Charleston, South Carolina, my cooking lessons began. It was then that I learned my most cherished skill: how to fry an egg. After finally mastering the art of flipping an egg while using a spatula the size of my arm, I was officially "a chef." The feeling of autonomy was intoxicating - I was buoyed by the certainty that if I was suddenly thrust out of my house at the ripe old age of 10, I could survive indefinitely on the fruits of my own labor (in this case, fried eggs and Capri Sun.) But no abandonment was necessary for me to zealously wield my newfound power; I simply had to make bi-weekly bike rides to the local Piggly Wiggly to keep our fridge stocked with eggs.

I was so proud of my abilities that I would only eat the food that I had prepared myself. My mother had unknowingly created the Cookie Monster of scrambled eggs. Though perhaps I owe my tall stature (a lofty 5'11" that I achieved by eighth grade) to my pure protein diet during the time of a major growth spurt, I can assure you that only eating eggs for an entire summer does not bode well with the stomach. Oh, the sacrifices we make to relish in our independence. Though triumphs of self-reliance and debacles of gastrointestinal distress aside, the real tool my mother had given me was creative license. Soon, I started experimenting with my homogenous diet. I started garnishing my eggs with salt and pepper, adding some shredded cheese, even making an "omelette-a-la-[author's name]," (which was just a flat pancake of whisked eggs.) My eyes were opened to the world of artistic expression through food.

Years later, I, a seventh grade Iron Chef, would prove my years of skill in preparing the menu for Mother's Day. A homemade cake with bittersweet chocolate icing and pink fondant hearts was perched on our cake stand under a glass lid as I began preparing breakfast, busily squeezing oranges and brewing hot tea. I expertly added a dollop of ricotta and orange zest to my pancake batter, and set the table with our fine silver cutlery and the napkins I had ironed the night before. Soon dinner was looming closer and closer, the crown jewel of the day. Hand-rolled gnocchi filled the house with its aroma, and the bittersweet chocolate from the cake added the perfect tang to end my day as an epicure. Though I thought the pancakes weren't quite soft enough, or the cake was a bit lopsided, my mother assured me it was the best day she had ever had. And while she was most likely just humoring me, I like to think that she tasted the love in the food rather than just the food itself.

I take after my mother by expressing my love through food; "food is a celebration of our blessings," she always says. I've learned that in any expression of art, strong feelings yield strong results. Though the path to find this out may have been unconventional and albeit a little gassy at times, I will never forget the humid day in a Charleston summer when a young chef was born.

Analysis

This beautifully written essay incorporates highly descriptive imagery and a terrific voice to give us a sense of who this student is. The readers are able to picture the author struggling in the kitchen "flipping an egg while using a spatula the size of my arm" and feel the care and love that goes into preparing the cake that "was a bit lopsided." The sentiment that "strong feelings yield strong results" is a testament to this student's passion for their pursuits and their dedication to the activities in which they invest their time.

Tangents
Josh Vandervelde

I'm a half-Asian kid whose parents practically speak the languages of mathematics and physics. When I say I'm in love with tangents, what else could I mean than those darn useful lines that brush against curves? Well, I'm in love with communicational tangents, the ones that veer conversation a tad off topic. *Hmm... I do suppose both tangents diverge from their original path, so they're not really that different...* Anyways.

I've found that tangents are often treated like unappetizing food: they're unwelcome at the table, can be hard to swallow, and make you want to return to the rest of your meal *very* quickly. In other words, people just don't like them. When I go off on tangents, I try not to blather on about grotesquely unrelated topics: I slip in small remarks, most of which are tied to the chat. On one occasion, though, I may have gone too far with my college counselor, Jaime.

"Josh, you need to choose a concrete topic you can write passionately about. The only ends we've come to so far are the ends of tangential loops you keep going off on."

Loops, loops like the wheels of the bicycle passing by our window, two conversations going around and around together but on two separate axes...

"Sorry." I respond, sounding guilty. "I only seem to go off on tangents with a handful of people."

"Why do you think so?" She sounds genuinely curious.

Interesting question. I like it. Maybe it's due to the freedom our chat allows. It's not a straightforward, academic setting but nor is it without structure, allowing for creative improvisation...

Jaime checks her watch.

...right, she does need to leave soon. I suppose I'll be direct and wrap this conversation up.

To me, tasty tangents are like twisting tunnels: the more you poke around, the more discoveries you make. Unfortunately, most people don't like wandering aimlessly on paths of conversation. Their eyes are set straight ahead, determined to reach a concrete conclusion to their communication; any deviations from said path are annoyances. And I understand, communication in our society is largely about sharing ideas, not creating them.

But in my opinion, tunnels of conversation are so much more engaging when you metaphorically discover the trickling cave creek, that grove of pinkish moss, those slumbering bats hanging from stalactite. Curiosity drives exploration, and for me, tangents are a way to verbally express my curiosity.

Tangents aren't always counterproductive as well, contrary to common belief.

Just as deviating from a central tunnel system may lead a group of wanderers somewhere wonderfully unexpected, conversational tangents have led me to devise some of my most creative ideas.

Six months ago, I was discussing with my biology teacher the possibility of replacing much of our science building's artificial light with self-sustaining bioluminescent light.

Wondering aloud, I questioned how the essential function of living plant light would differ from solar panel light, save for materials. Tangential thought locked and loaded, my imagination began replacing living cells with solar cells, the leafy plant structure with a semi translucent plastic one, and the proteins responsible for bioluminescent glow with small LEDs. Hexagonally shaped, the concept—which I later named Plantern—was designed so when it sensed light, its plastic petals would bloom open, allowing an internal solar panel to convert the sun's energy into stored energy.

When night fell, the petals would huddle to a close, using that day's energy to power LEDs and illuminate its surroundings. Since then, I have physically prototyped my Plantern, fixed kinks in the design, and hope to see it propagate across campus before I graduate. But anyways, back to the matter of tangents.

Sure I can be straightforward when I need to be. Sure some people may not enjoy veering off topic. But creativity and curiosity are essential parts of my identity, and when I can express them, I will. *Speaking of which...*

Analysis

Humor and personality are plentiful in this essay, and the student's creative use of tangents as a jumping off point to describe their curiosity proves to be effective.

The student's astute observation that "communication in our society is largely about sharing ideas, not creating them" shows us that they have an inner desire to innovate. The second half of this essay gives us a glimpse into the student's creativity and problem-solving skills through their creation of the "Plantern."

Breath
Anonymous

When I was younger, I used to ask my Dad - as children do - "when will I be grown up?" Each time his answer would be the same: "It's not about age, it's not about size or strength, it'll be when you're ready to take responsibility". Well, you want to know what responsibility is? It's when someone hands you a Bag Valve Mask and tells you "here, you need to breathe for this man."

The back of an ambulance with blasting lights and sirens can be a very eerie place. Reflections of red and blue light bounce in through the window, dancing around the empty cabin. As they pass over the airway cabinet I begin to hear, very clearly, my own breathing. And when the radio strapped to my belt crackles to life, followed by the voice of the dispatcher announcing, "CPR in progress", I hear my heart beating as well.

The door to the house is already open. We turn into the living room, where a policeman is kneeling by the side of a man's body, surrounded on 3 sides by black leather sofas. The walls seem very close together. My partner and I move a Christmas tree out of the way. Within seconds I take the place of the policeman and begin compressions. The purple of my gloved hands - fingers interlocked, palms down - stands out against the dark green of a woolen sweater vest. It looks new - a present, maybe.

After four cycles of CPR my partner and I switch places- I quickly move towards the man's head to continue rescue breathing. My boot slips for a second. I glance down and see a small brown gift bag. On it, a label stands out. *His name.* Suddenly, everything stops. This man is about to die. The air turns thick, like the room's filling with sea foam - so heavy you can't move or breathe or think anymore. Just before it swallows me up my partner's voice snaps me to with the most beautiful four words an EMT can hear: "We have a pulse."

Looking down I put a face to the name. He's real. Around him hang pictures of his real family and I can feel the pressure of their real eyes on my skin, the weight of a world - his world - on my shoulders. They've put their trust in me and right here, right now, I have a responsibility to earn it. I reach out and take the Bag Valve Mask from my partner.

In a blur he's on the stretcher, out the door, and in the back of the ambulance. For the time it takes to get to the hospital, it's my family in the pictures on the living room wall. Over the screaming of sirens and the rumbling of the undercarriage I once again find myself listening to the sound of breathing. But this time it's someone else's.

When my crew and I step out of the Emergency Room, we're all silent. Nobody wants to get back into the ambulance just yet. Instead, we stand there and take a moment to breathe, bathed in the soft red glow of the ER sign. I don't think I'll ever be comfortable in front of a dead body. I don't ever want to be. But it's during these uncomfortable moments that I've learned to tell myself, "Right now, you're a part of something bigger than yourself. You have a job to do - get it done". That night, it was the only choice I had. I proved - if only to myself - that when it matters most, I'm ready to take responsibility.

Analysis

This essay presents an outstanding story about a unique and harrowing experience. Although this essay is packed with action, this student has made sure to include details that show qualities of their character. We witness this student's maturity and ability to confront the difficult aspects of life with courage. The theme of responsibility that runs through the entire essay gives us the sense that this student will confidently take on their future work with poise. Also, as the student recounts their experience, they show that they empathize with the patient, and at the end, they show that experiences like these have prepared them to be responsible. Most students will not have a story like this, but for those who do, this essay serves as an example on how to present a clean and coherent narrative.

The Power of Listening
Anonymous

"What is LGBTQ?" my mother and I asked Google. We sat silently in front of the computer, waiting for an answer.

Earlier that day, I received a questionnaire from the study abroad organization. It contained just a single question: do you have any concerns with being placed in a home with a bisexual young woman? My mother and I stared at each other, confused about what we had just read. In Japan, we do not openly discuss LGBTQ issues. People are aware that such individuals exist, but only in movies or on television shows and usually as figures for comedic relief or ridicule.

So, when I arrived in Newport, Oregon a few months later, I was nervous. I had never encountered a bisexual person in my life. What kind of person would I meet? Will she be different from a straight person? Will I do something that offends her? Will she fall in love with me? I reassured myself thinking that things will be just 'a little' different from the relationship my sister and I had back in Japan.

Living with Winter, my bisexual host sister, was far from just 'a little' different. It was surprisingly mundane. We shared our favorite music and watched Star Wars movies. We had serious conversations about cultural differences between the United States and Japan. We supported each other when the other was down - usually through stuffed animals fights or a sarcastic joke.

However, I learned that Winter's life was not as

normal as it seemed. My host family confided in me Winter's difficult experiences from her childhood. Her own family had trouble accepting Winter's sexuality. Winter was bullied in elementary school, which led her to leave and be home-schooled until high school.

To support her daughter through this difficult period, Winter's mother began to take part in their community's LGBTQ support group, and eventually served as the chairperson. On Monday evenings, I accompanied her to learn more about how I could better support Winter and the community she belonged to. I watched Winter's mother and was confused by the scene. She simply sat and listened to the stories being shared. I began to wonder if she was actually supporting these individuals. Where was the action?

As the meeting continued, I began to reflect on the other activities my host mother worked on. I realized that all of her work, whether it was advocating for gender neutral bathrooms or hosting LGBTQ workshops at other schools, were rooted in the stories that she had heard. By listening, she conveyed both empowerment and empathy. More importantly, she was not positioning herself at the center of this struggle. She was taking action on behalf of the LGBTQ community.

To genuinely support Winter and her community, I realized I would need to listen and shape my actions based on their experiences and insights. After moving back to Japan, I sought out the stories of the Japanese LGBTQ community. When my friends and I marched at the Tokyo Rainbow Pride Parade, I used it as an opportunity to not just visibly show my support, but to also interact with individuals marching in it and hear their stories. To refine my understanding of LGBTQ issues and to share the stories of this community with others, I pursued an independent research project at my school that traced the development of sexual norms in Japan.

The time I spent with Winter and her family was truly valuable. From my time together with Winter and her family, I learned that creating meaningful change does not always require taking visible action. Rather, it is listening, sharing, empathy and acceptance that will allow me to be a true ally for the individuals and communities I love.

Analysis

This essay illustrates this student's ability to connect with an individual that comes from a distinctly different background than they do. This essay does a great job of showing this person's care for social justice. The author highlights the importance of understanding in uplifting a discriminated community. The student describes how they've taken an initiative to learn more about LGBTQ issues and immerse themselves in their community. The closing paragraph ties everything together by demonstrating that through listening we demonstrate love

Discovering My Perspective
Anonymous

Bows moved in uniform as our fingers jumped toward the higher registers of our violins. I, along with 204 other musicians, sat in the Iowa All-State Orchestra Performance Hall playing Shostakovich's *Fifth Symphony*. The brass trumpeted the might of the Red Army, and the melodies of the flutes tip-toed under the "watchful eyes" of Joseph Stalin. As the last chord rang through the hall, the conductor waved down his baton and said, "Shostakovich was ordered to portray the glory of the Soviet Union." However, we later learned that the subtle nuances in the music actually reflected Shostakovich's resentment towards the oppressive totalitarian government. His music conveyed a perspective that was completely new to me. I never could have imagined that after performing this piece, my life would be intertwined with a culture that built St. Petersburg, started socialism, and gave us Vladimir Putin.

That performance engraved a deep impression on me. A week after All-State, a quick Google search on "Soviet music" brought up pictures of Lenin statues, red stars, and a strange alphabet with backward "Rs." Months later, I found myself walking beneath the arches of Pembroke Hall on my way to my first summer Russian language class at Bryn Mawr College. A wide-eyed 15-year-old, I was unsure if I could stomach both independent living and six grammar cases. Fast forward three years, I exited the gates on 116th and Broadway having finished my final exam of Advanced Russian at Columbia University. After all these years of encountering Russian culture, I continue to be amazed by the hooligans in the film

Stilyagi, the drawbridges along Nevsky Prospekt, and the lessons of morality in *Crime and Punishment*.

Given my fascination with Russian culture, the most impactful moment was when I bumped into Diana Popova in the halls of my school during my junior year. When I first learned she was a Ukrainian foreign exchange student, I was overjoyed. We immediately became friends. After all, finding another Russian speaker in my small, Iowa town was hard enough (even if neither of us were actually Russian).

Diana came from Donetsk, where war had threatened the security of her family everyday. She and I would often talk about her home and the turmoil happening in eastern Ukraine. After meeting her, I started to read more about the conflict on both Russian and American news outlets. I quickly ascertained that they differed not only in language, but also in outlook. Once again, I recognized the importance of perspective, which I encountered playing the *Fifth Symphony*. I identified the gap between the reality I heard from Diana and the reports I read on these news outlets, and I formed my own perspective. I felt obligated to disclose the narratives Diana shared with me because her stories revealed that the voices of Ukrainian people were being silenced. Since then, my perspective became a powerful tool because it was my motivation to tell the unfiltered stories of Diana and countless other Ukrainians without the fear of politically-charged consequences. In many ways, the melodies in Shostakovich's *Fifth Symphony* that I played three years ago now took on a new meaning as I looked at pictures of Maidan Square covered in smoke.

My awareness of the privilege that comes with my position– from being able to experience playing a politically-crafted symphony to befriending Diana– started out with studying the Russian language. I continue to draw strength from my language studies, building connections through cross-cultural experiences. Perhaps my study of the Russian language will allow me to continue recognizing the untold stories of the Ukrainian people. Or perhaps my study of the Russian language will broaden my horizons and shape my life in ways unimaginable to me right now. Most importantly, I am full of excitement, knowing that my perspective can motivate me to engrave a truth in the face of injustice, one thought at a time.

Analysis

This essay presents a unique perspective from a student raised in a small, Iowa town interested in Russian culture. What makes this essay so effective is that there are strong examples and experiences that confirm their interest in Russian culture, from their summer Russian language courses to befriending another Russian speaker in their town. This student's desire to become more aware of global issues, specifically in Ukraine, demonstrates their genuine passion to discover different perspectives. The closing paragraph is strong because it charts out future steps and gives us a sense of what the author will continue to achieve in the future.

More Than Outcomes
Anonymous

My piano teacher looked at me with some pleasure but mostly amazement. I had just agreed to perform in the recital.

I was even more surprised. Although in the past I had performed for a few elderly couples privately and held an occasional "concert" at a local nursing home, few had ever heard me play the piano. In fact, most didn't even know that I could play at all.

So in the following days I often wondered if I was prepared to perform a recital in front of so many people. The last time I left my shell was in the fifth grade talent show, when I froze up in the middle of my piece and couldn't remember what came next. Perhaps, I thought, history is doomed to repeat itself.

Trying to ignore my doubts, I did the only thing I knew to do: practice. I practiced feverishly, sometimes for four hours a day. In two weeks, my teacher told me the piece was ready. I didn't listen, and in another two weeks, she told me it was almost perfect.

Even though I had all the notes right, I now felt I had to get the perfect tone, expression, and articulation; my practice time only increased. I was driving myself into the ground.

I decided to take off the day before the recital to rest. That's when I started to reflect: "Why am I obsessing over this? To correct the past? To show off my abilities? To prove myself to myself?"

Probably all three.

But I came to realize that what really mattered was that in my frantic pursuit of perfection I had lost sight of the joy that music brings and the gift of experiencing it.

Music isn't just a set of notes to learn and perform. Music is when my heart spills out of my fingers and sings its deepest pains and joys and fears. It's where I lay myself and my burdens before God and I feel his healing embrace. It's when my suppressed emotions awake in full, without reservation. In short, music is when I am free.

And I was letting it enslave me.

So on that day I chose to unshoulder the fears that were weighing me to the ground.

Perfectionism may sometimes bring the desired results, but never fulfillment. Not just for some recital but for life in general. I'm not concerned about my test scores or a perfect GPA or even if I get accepted into a great school. My life is not defined by my achievements. All those things are great, but there is far more joy in growth and learning.

But I would be remiss to not tell you the rest of the story.

I rose to the stage and headed for the piano. As I sat down and began playing, I felt my heart keep time with the piece's slow, steady tempo. Soon I was lost in the music and the audience disappeared. I was completely alone. The anguish and passion in the notes and the complex emotions pent up inside me harmonized to form a poignancy within that can only be described as deeply spiritual. For the first time in a long time I experienced music, and somehow understood life more truly.

I returned to an enthusiastic applause. And the best part: it made no difference.

Analysis

A tightly written, cohesive narrative, this essay is one that demonstrates maturity and deep self-awareness. This student's reflection that "perfectionism may sometimes bring the desired results, but never fulfillment" is particularly insightful. As the essay progresses, readers get the sense that the author has established a balance between always striving for excellence and finding joy and peace through the process. The essay doesn't try too hard to impress us with achievements or overly intellectual writing, but instead clearly presents the student's values and character, which is precisely what writers should aim to do in the personal statement.

What Writing Means To Me
Christine Park

I wiped my sweaty palms on my jeans. I could feel my heavy, irregular breathing. I attempted to silence my thumping heart out of worry that my friends might hear.

Releasing a long sigh, I tried to relax as I closed my eyes.

"Congratulations to Christine Park from Irvine, California for winning the Excellence Award for the 2017 National High School Journalism Convention sports write-offs!" My eyes popped open. Wait a minute! I'm Christine Park from Irvine! I won!

Rewind to a few days back.

My journalism teacher began our daily 7:00 A.M. zero period class with reports of current events. But before telling us to continue working on the publication, she said, "This year, the annual national convention will be in Dallas, Texas. The first eight people—"

"Can I?" I shouted enthusiastically. Before my teacher could even finish her sentence, my hand bolted into the air.

I couldn't take the Beginning Journalism class in my freshman year because of schedule conflicts. The year I wasted was more like a million missed opportunities. However, I believe in the philosophy that everything happens for a reason. Because I missed so much, I made it my mission to open every door of opportunity presented to me. I maximized the benefits this class offered me to become the overzealous sponge of journalism.

Since I was young, I loved writing. It takes a while for me to organize my thoughts while I'm talking, but when I write, my pencil becomes a brush on canvas and my writing the masterpiece.

Over the years, my appearance changed. My handwriting changed. My opinions changed. But writing remained my outlet. When I had to rant but didn't want to be a bother, I wrote in my journals. Because I am the only one who reads my journals, I don't have to wear a mask. I could be me.

Practice doesn't make perfect, but it does make better. And as my writing improved over the years, I wanted to share it with my community. So when I learned about the internationally-acknowledged journalism program my high school had, I knew it would be the next step to progress my passion.

But never did I imagine my sports stories would be the most sought-after section in the school newspaper. Never did I imagine I would receive awards for my writing.
It felt great— no, better than great— to receive validation from peers, judges, and teachers for doing what I love.

I am not in charge of many things in my life. But when I write, I control every word choice, sentence structure, paragraph length, and even the strokes of each letter. As I write how the day went, a panorama of my day flashes. And that becomes the story I write— my story. Writing is meaningful to me because it gives me something that is my own.

Analysis

This essay is a great example of how to write about an activity you're deeply involved with. We see this student's motivations for writing (the ability to have a sense of ownership and define their life) and commitment to excellence (the awards they've received). The little details like "overzealous sponge of journalism" give us the sense that this student will dive headfirst into whatever they are involved with. Through this essay, we are able to see that this author is driven, bold, and eager. Remember that elements pertaining to character, personality, and drive are key. We also witness their commitment to growth ("Practice doesn't make perfect...") and genuine passion for journalism that helps us get to know them.

Learning By Debating
Anonymous

I couldn't believe it. Nueva Upper School, in just its third month of existence, had mandated yet another seminar on racial privilege. The discussion quickly devolved into arguing against the students with overtly racist opinions. Why was I here? I was socially liberal and had a diverse background (Palestinian, Japanese, and Lithuanian) — I wasn't a racist.

Two years later, I found myself preparing for that month's debate team topic: reparations for African Americans. As I dove into the literature, I stumbled upon a book that thoroughly critiqued my colorblind worldview. I discovered that 21st century racism operates covertly, protecting white privilege and masking institutional injustice by convincing individuals like me that we hold no implicit biases. Appalled by my ignorance, I pushed further, eventually reaching the conclusion that I couldn't be taught in any well-meaning seminar: I, given my white skin, was complicit in our country's longstanding system of oppression. I felt ashamed that I had ever doubted the prevalence of institutional racism in modern society. Yet, I also recognized that, in this case, my school's attempts to inform me of my white privilege had failed: only through pursuing the knowledge myself could I truly grasp the extent to which racism persists.

I found that I fell in love with debate for just that reason: for me, knowledge is most meaningful when I seek it out myself. Despite my love and passion for the activity, however, I soon realized that the debate community itself struggles with exclusivity and privilege. The 2016 Tournament of Champions taught me this most directly. My debate partner and I spent several months developing a position on making public infrastructure accessible to people of all abilities; we had interviewed civil rights lawyers, talked to fellow debaters with disabilities, and spent hours researching the subject.

We argued that inaccessible infrastructure is what creates disability in the first place — individuals are only disabled as long as the built environment prevents them from executing functions "fully-abled" people can perform.

While I found the argument compelling, most judges at the tournament felt otherwise. Many voted against us on the grounds of "not liking" our argument or "not being convinced disabled people mattered." By the conclusion of the tournament, I discovered that debate, despite all it means to me, is not always the open, accepting community I had envisioned it to be. Low-income students and racial minorities are excluded, women are criticized more for the tone of their voice and the length of their dress than the quality of their arguments, and matters of ability are routinely cast aside. While tackling oppression in broader society seems daunting, I hope I can address at least some of the problems within the debate community. After all, debate has changed my life: I went from a kid who attended school because it was expected of him to an individual who, unafraid to think critically and challenge the status-quo, learns because he loves the thrill of discovery.

One necessary step is improving debate's accessibility. This summer, I had the opportunity to teach at the Bay Area Urban Debate League, an organization with a mission to help underprivileged students find their voice through the activity. Expanding urban debate leagues nationally can play a huge role in increasing inclusivity.

Yet, we must also tackle biases within the community itself. It's on each of us to call out acts of bigotry at tournaments, whether the culprit is a judge, coach, or competitor. For our team, this also means recruiting more girls to debate and ensuring their voices are heard equally. We've additionally established a new mentorship program that I will continue to use to educate new members about the problems, not just the high points, of debate. Even if these steps only have a small impact on a large, complex issue, the outlook remains promising: I'm confident that debaters are always up to face a challenge.

Analysis

This essay possesses a rapid pace and covers a lot of ground in the space allotted— characteristic of a debater. The writing style avoids overly flowery prose, and stands out for its clarity and logical flow. The student's intellectual curiosity is on full display when they describe that their passion for debate stems from knowledge being "most meaningful when I seek it out myself," illustrating this with their investigation of how debate struggles with "exclusivity and privilege." Beyond seeking knowledge, we see that this student takes action and is a leader through their establishment of a debate league for underprivileged students.

The Growing Pains of Poetry
Anonymous

Poetry pains me. When I read great verses, I feel them inside me, like a cross between cardiac arrest and menstrual cramps. I feel brilliantly sad poems, poems that fly, poems built from words so gorgeous that I speak them out loud, tasting them on my tongue. Words like fluidity. Virtuoso. *Cantankerous.* Funnily enough, my favorite word is semantics. I savor each vocable, the way the letters translate into voice. I'm basically a word pervert.

Words give me a thrill, but the way they are arranged makes me shiver. It's the difference between beach glass collector and mosaic artist. "Let us go then, you and I, when the evening is spread out against the sky like a patient etherized upon a table." I could hear those lines in a smoker's grating voice and still fall in love. T.S. Eliot tortures my artistic soul.

When great poetry graces my ears, it's not the words themselves that cause my suffering, but rather the desire they instill: the desire to create. Inspiration flutters up inside me, her buttery wings rattling my ribcage, while Ambition squelches and croaks, hopping madly down my throat. They want desperately to relieve me of these words all jumbled and compressed within me and cannot rest until I put them to page. Writing is my catharsis, a release of the tension created by frustratingly beautiful poems.

Each time I write a "nice" one I think, "This is it! The best poem there is!" But no matter how lyrically I think I wax, there will always be lovelier poems to come along and obliterate my previous convictions. I've tried at poeticism for as long as I can remember. Imagine: fourth-grade me sits at an old desktop PC, constructing poetry one letter at a time with a steady tap-tap rhythm. I am writing about hot chocolate. I know that good poetry, however, must be about more than my favorite drink; hot chocolate is a metaphor.

> When my cocoa is cool, I lick, sip and gulp it
> And after I'm done, I ask my mom,
> "What's the secret ingredient?"
> My mom answers,
> "Patience."

My fourth-grade self apparently understood, but patience is something that I am still learning. Poems, like anything in life, are not permanent; they require tender dedication, someone to care for them over the years. As Paul Valéry said, "A poem is never finished, only abandoned." My poem may be dusty from eight years of abandonment, but it can be revived with revision and a fresh coat of paint. As I look now on my modest little poem, I would replace "when my cocoa is cool" for a more vivid descriptor, like "when the steam has ghosted off, leaving layers of soft froth." I would delete the second line, and add a few words to the end. "I find the recipe / not in words / but in the spaces between, / the pause / that speaks without voice, / that is without cause."

I continue to grow and, much like my poems, my evolution is nonlinear. There is no end goal, no absolute understanding to be reached. My poems simply aim to make the reader feel, to express the pain and joy of writing in finite language. Through combinations of twenty-six letters, poems can capture the intensity and breadth of human emotions. I can make others laugh, hurt, and wonder as I do. I can connect. So, I will try to explain my self in the language I know best and build a bridge to reach my reader across the nation. Here is me, packaged into ars poetica on a computer screen.

Poems whirl and weave like dervish dancers.
Poems are not wise or set in stone commandment.
They are more curve than point,
more question than answer.
They are not given or bought,
but borrowed and lent.
They are word-lust and pain
that scream longer, louder.

Poems are sweet, cheap,
chocolate packet powder.

Analysis

This essay establishes the student as a highly skilled and intelligent writer. It clearly showcases the student's passion for poetry. Humor also shines through in this essay ("I'm basically a word pervert"), as well as other character traits such as the desire for constant improvement ("There is no end goal, no absolute understanding to be reached"). Most powerfully, the students edits their own poem during the essay, showing their self-awareness and growth. The essay also ends with a short, original poem that further affirms the student's mastery of their craft.

A Song of Love
Maya Plotnick

All 29 of us headed to a meeting room for our evening activity at the University of Chicago's floChicago (Future Leaders of Chicago) program, a weeklong leadership program for rising seniors that focuses on how to take action within various social justice issues. When we were waiting for the activity to start, I stood at the outskirts of the group, everyone crowding around the piano to the left of the glass door. One guy was fiercely banging out a classical piece full of runs and big chords and speedy figures. When he finished playing, the room erupted in loud clapping and cheers. I clapped along, and itched to sit on that bench and give the keys a run of my own. I didn't say a word, about to walk away, when Matt, the founder of floChicago, called out for me to play.

I was grateful for his encouragement, and I walked over to the piano bench and sat down. My feet reached for the pedals like they've done countless times before, even though I knew I didn't need them for the song I was about to play. I had taught myself the piano part to "Love Song" by Sara Bareilles after hearing it for the first time in sixth grade. The opening four measures are the most recognizable part of the song- a series of chords that isn't very challenging, but music doesn't need to be hard to have emotion. Even though the lyrics are sassy, the chords are warm and strong. The message could be conveyed without singing a word.

As I played the first chord, I could hear sporadic gasps from all around me. A smile formed on my face because one of my favorite parts of music is making others feel included. I get the same feeling in choir- every note that's sung takes the entire group's effort to complete. As the song progressed that night at floChicago, so did the volume of singing voices, and my fingers became more determined with each strike of the keys. I listened around the room, and I recognized that not only was everyone singing along, but I could hear every single smile.

These moments when I'm able to lift people's spirit up with music inspire me because I can positively impact someone through a hobby that I love, which is so rewarding. At floChicago, a few simple, familiar chords filled the room with feelings of belonging and community. I'm in awe of the ability of music to make people happy.

Music is enjoyable because it requires a balance of self-fulfillment and fulfilling others. I've experienced the culmination of this balance at Blue Lake Fine Arts Camp, which I've attended for five summers. After 12 exhausting days of rehearsal, the campers give a final performance for families and friends. My voice was shot from almost 70 hours of rehearsal, but finally showcasing our singing and making our parents happy and proud made all of our practice worthwhile.

For the past 12 years of music study, my teachers have taught me to conquer sonatas, rhapsodies, and arias. In the future, I'll still turn to my instructors to help me grow as a musician. I turn to the audience to learn why music is important. My parents, friends, fellow music students, and even strangers teach me how to play and sing with purpose. Performing for myself is only half the motivation; performing for my community is when music becomes truly meaningful. My peers at floChicago taught me that nothing compares to bringing people together with a song. Who knew that Bareilles's decade-old pop hit would become a classic in my music repertoire.

Analysis

An easy and pleasant read, this essay draws upon the simple joy of good music that brings people together. The opening story of the student playing piano in the floChicago program is captivating primarily due to the imagery and details like "my feet reached for the pedals" and "I could hear every single smile." The author also skillfully explains their love for music — "it requires a balance of self-fulfillment and fulfilling others." This essay doesn't try to do too much and that is its strength. We see that this student is a kind individual who values community and has found her way of creating it through music—exactly what a liberal arts school is looking for.

Dancing Through Time
Atticus Maloney

Take in a deep breath. Exhale out stress. The breath continues twisting; it is the embodiment of rhythmic movement. Dance is my release from fear, the catalyst to my academic success, and the root for my love of meditation. I started dancing when I was ten years old. Unfortunately, this activity is still considered a smidgen strange for a male in rural Maine. Due to my large frame, I was expected to play football, but even the action of picking the uniform filled me with dread. Dance had the opposite effect.

In middle school, dance was my only form of self-expression. I transferred from a Montessori school with fewer than fifty kids to a public school of one thousand. Honestly, it was terrifying. It was a transition from the social equivalent of singing Kumbaya to a world of popularity, insults, and crushes. I refused to speak outside of class, fearing I was not adequate enough to have friends.

Dance is my respite from fear. When I dance — contemporary, ballet, tap, tango, you name it — I can feel my whole body, every muscle and tendon, energized and alive. Not an escape, but an embrace of the things that scare me the most.

My relationship with dance was forever changed by my decision to go to the Maine School of Science and Mathematics (MSSM)- Maine's only public, boarding, magnet high school. Previously in school I had an average over one hundred, I was on track to be salutatorian, and I was dancing for six hours a day. I was at the top of all my games, but my mind felt like it was doing the equivalent of endless pivot turns. I wanted to push the extent of my mental abilities. More than that, I wanted to find a community where I could express all my selves, where I wouldn't be afraid to speak.

So there I was: lying on the ground after my first week of classes at MSSM, more afraid than ever, flattened to the floor by the weight of my stresses. How could I have given up my amazing dance program and easy A's to come to this godforsaken school in the middle of nowhere?

Stubbornly, I lay there...and began to notice my breathing. In. Out. I began to remember why I had come to this school. It *was* a crazy decision, neglecting both practicality and comfort, but I had wanted to explore what was possible. I had hated resting on my abilities; I wanted to see how far they could each be pushed. Through the breath, I rediscovered my motivation. I was aware of two things in that moment: I was going to be just fine at MSSM and I loved the silence of breathing.

Meditation is watching my mind's internal dance to the beat of the breath. It became, and still is, my way to dance through academic rigor. Through breathing's gentle adagio, I learned to calm down enough to ask questions—lots and lots of them. I pestered my teachers, my friends, and student tutors, trying to perform the rigorous ballet of effective studying. My skills eventually improved and I was named an MSSM "Renaissance man." Most importantly, I have been given the opportunity, both as a Residential Assistant and as a student tutor, to instruct new students in MSSM's dance of learning.

With every breath, I am extremely grateful to MSSM's community. I have tried to reciprocate with my most valuable treasure: dance. Walk into the gymnasium Saturday afternoon and you will see MSSM's first dance club; twelve dedicated students and one crazily enthusiastic president — me. I love that I have been able to bring movement and art to a school of video games and mathematical precision. What's next? Bringing art and movement into the STEM fields. When technology and grace combine, a new creation will be born.

Analysis

This writer's description of dance as a mode of expression oozes passion and energy. We learn that dance is more than an activity— it's a way of being ("I can feel my whole body.... energized and alive") for the student. "Watching my mind's internal dance to the beat of the breath" is a nice use of figurative language that sets up the student's journey to finding their place in a new environment. This essay does a phenomenal job in all three categories of PAR— personality, action, and reflection. Readers are confident that this writer has grit and maturity; the author demonstrates that they are able to manage their emotions effectively and exercise mental calm in the face of challenge and rapid change. The closing paragraph is particularly strong, establishing the student as a leader organizing an activity they are passionate about and a creative thinker who sees exciting new possibilities.

You Need to Chili
Sandy Shen

Nanny. *Ah po.* Angry bird. My mom's nicknames for me have always been, to say the least, a bit too accurate about my personality. Whenever she calls me Nanny, I know she will admonish me for nagging my little brother too much about his homework; whenever she calls me *ah po* (little granny), I know she will chastise me for being too blunt about my dad's hygiene; whenever she calls me angry bird, I know she must be comparing me to the puffy red bird in Angry Birds. Yet regardless of the context, she will always follow up each nickname with something along the lines of "you need to let go" or "you don't need to be so serious." But no matter how many different names she called me by, I never thought to reconsider what she meant. To me, my independent nature and serious streak were prized assets that I had spent years cultivating.

Since I was a child, I believed there was no one better to count on than myself; relying on others meant risking disappointment, false hope, and empty promises -- everything my mom warned me of. And as she drove me to school and viola lessons, she never failed to reinforce her advice: "never rely on a man," "make sure you always have something to fall back on," and "don't end up like me." It was listening to her stories, watching tears trickle down her face in the rearview mirror, that made me realize how suffocating and stifling an unbalanced marriage could be. The very idea of being locked in a cage, bound by love and familial obligation, truly terrified me, and it was more than enough to cement my willful independence in everything I did for years to come.

Yet one day in high school, as I reached for a pre-made bag of brownie mix, I wondered what I was doing. Two years ago, I would have pulled out my buckets of flour and sugar, ready to whip up a tray of fudgy brownies from scratch. But now, I realized I hadn't baked in years -- the only time I had in between meetings, homework, and lessons was for eating and sleeping. When had I forgotten my passion for baking? When had my personality become so extreme? When had my fixation with self-determination become a sign to take sole responsibility for group efforts?

In retrospect, my stubborn streak propelled me forward in schoolwork and extracurriculars, pushing me to initiate conversations with teachers, learn material on my own, and create fundraisers and activities. But at that moment, as I saw all of the boxes of ready-to-use brownie mix lined up in the pantry, disappointment welled up inside of me. All my efforts to be different from my parents, to ensure that I became a balanced, self-sustaining adult, had led me to create an unsustainable relationship with control. Finally, my mom's words of advice -- "let go, move on, don't be so serious" -- took on new meaning. Instead of plowing through everything on my own, never stopping to relish the moment or consider others' opinions, I needed to invest in the people around me. Otherwise, everything I had worked so hard to build would crumble -- after all, I was only one person.

The transition from a hard-headed child to a more open, receptive leader felt foreign, even invasive. Yet as I learned to "let go," to accept the risks that come with trusting others, I felt my days lighten. As I delegated tasks, allowing others to rise, I could focus on editing websites and scouting speakers while still leaving time to bake and draw. Even my mom, having noticed my rekindled passion for banana bread and madeleines, rewarded me with another nickname: "chili," to honor my newfound vigor and brightness.

Analysis

In this essay, the student discusses their journey in learning how to share responsibility and become a better leader. The opening paragraphs establish a detailed background about the student and give us a good sense of their independent personality. Nicknames are a great way to add originality and flavor to an essay. From the get-go, we understand a key aspect of the author's personality: that they are bold, independent, and self-serious.

However, we are most impressed by their reflections later in the essay when they acknowledge how their self-reliant attitude has become destructive ("When had my personality become so extreme..."). There is a genuine sense of transformation, when the author walks readers through her thought process in the third and fourth paragraphs. She is able to use baking to illustrate this transformation. Readers are able to see that the author is self aware and able to take a step back to reflect. Particularly impressive is the author's ability to deliberately make a change (albeit small) in their mindset, which influences their behaviors in daily life.

Never Again A Zero Day
Sam Shih

I performed a perfect sleight of hand and asked her to kiss me. Did she notice the card's double-lift? Wait – she actually kissed me? My first kiss came spring of junior year with the clever climax of my "promposal" card-magic routine for Bridgette. As I handed her the roses, I marveled at how far I'd progressed.

Rewind to winter break. I had just flaked on dinner with friends, opting to play League of Legends instead. Like most nights, I kept losing, unable to play with a clear head. I had quit going to the gym with the intention to learn code but ended up playing video games instead. Facing my reflection in the monitor every time I started a new round, I wondered — how had I gained so much weight?

A text from my friend that evening interrupted my pity party: "Have you seen this post on reddit?" I knew exactly which post he was talking about but had been avoiding reading about this college student's social dejection. Too close to home. Still, although I had accomplished nothing this break, I wanted to do something about it. I scrolled through the post, lingering over one phrase.

No more Zero Days. A Zero Day is when you don't do a single thing towards whatever dream or want you have. Productivity happens from a string of consistent non-Zero Days.

It was already getting late, but I didn't want that to be my excuse anymore. Without a minute to lose, I started my first non-Zero Day with push-ups, maxing my arms out at 10. In the following weeks, I continued with other small steps to improve my habits: play fewer video games, eat healthier food, and practice programming daily. After I felt more confident and productive, I tackled my bigger ambitions: mastering web development and making significant contributions as an intern at Caviar (a food delivery start-up). To achieve my goal, I shadowed the experienced engineers and participated in all optional marketing meetings. Then with Caviar's business model in mind, I built an auto-payout feature that saves Caviar $1,000/week and developed the web framework Caviar now uses to scale internationally.

After my internship, I had reached a programming level I was proud of, but holding eye-contact with girls still topped my list of awkward scenarios. So I followed YouTube tutorials to improve my social confidence - one smile, handshake and conversation at a time. Through my Red Cross activities, I challenged my fear of public speaking by leading the largest disaster presentation any CPR instructor has given. I then set out to help other students feel comfortable in the social situations that used to make me anxious. I dedicated meetings to connect face-to-face with the members at my club, growing closer to and developing more intimate friendships with them.

Looking back to my first non-Zero Day, all the things I've accomplished since proved to me that I can improve myself. I can now do over 80 push ups and got hired as an engineer by Square Inc.! I've even stepped up my game and took the prettiest girl at school to prom. Also, I was humbled to see that my improvement had inspired the peers around me. Together, members of my

Red Cross club raised over $12,000 for the victims of Typhoon Haiyan. But what I've learned from my journey is that self-improvement isn't defined by my individual successes — it is my lifestyle.

Never again a Zero Day.

Analysis

This essay showcases many of the writer's positive character traits, which help the reader envision how they might contribute to and succeed at Swarthmore. From their constant desire for growth ("Never again a Zero day") to their leadership ("members of my Red Cross club raised over $12,000 for the victims of Typhoon Haiyan") we get a sense that this writer is a driven and motivated individual. The opening paragraph utilizes a classic method called in medias res; it starts in the middle of the action to hook the reader and then goes back to explain how the story progressed to that point. From this essay we get the sense that the writer will go above and beyond with whatever they do.

In terms of the PAR framework, this essay does a particularly good job in the "Action" department. Be wary, though, of overloading the essay with "action" details; the purpose of these actions is to show the reader how you think, what your motivations are, and what your personality is like. The goal is not to rattle off a list of your achievements. Here, it makes sense to include achievements, because it relates directly to the theme of transformation from someone without direction to someone who is goal-oriented and accomplished.

The Importance of Imaginary People
Elizabeth Miller

All of my life I have been in love with stories. I was the kid who always begged for one last chapter before bed, and when my mom turned off the lights and left the room, I would pull out a flashlight and read for far too long under the covers. I was in love with imaginary people and the imaginary lives that they led, and I sought refuge in them and their perfect worlds. I'd always felt a distance between myself and my peers, and books gave me characters I could relate to and who made me feel less alone. Not only did they comfort me, but my favorite books and their characters helped create who I am.

At a young age, Hermione Granger taught me that a love of knowledge is nothing to be ashamed of; in fact, it is something to be celebrated. I learned from Atticus Finch that integrity will always be worth more than what others think of me. Lee from *East of Eden* instilled in me the true meaning of free will; he taught me that I control what path I take in life, regardless of my background. Holden Caulfield taught me that I am never alone in my struggles and frustrations, despite how isolated I may feel. My reading has given me real life heroes to emulate and learn from as well. Elie Wiesel gave me a complex portrait of the human soul and forced me to think deeply and critically about my world. Cheryl Strayed showed me strength and taught me how to build myself back up from rock bottom.

Even the villains I have grown to hate, the Voldemorts and the Cathy Ameses, have taught me invaluable lessons. They have shown me that while humans are capable of amazing, beautiful things, we are also capable of evil, and we should always be wary of that.

I see these characters in the tiny things I do everyday. I am reminded of Hermione as I hold my hand up proudly when I know the answer in my Chemistry class, even though I am greatly outnumbered by my male classmates. I try to imitate Atticus when I choose to speak from my heart about injustices I see instead of allowing myself to follow a crowd, while knowing that I will often go unheard. I hear Lee counseling me as I grapple with my self doubt while applying to colleges, despite the fact that neither of my parents have college degrees. I am Holden when I can't help but complain and view the world with a cynical eye, and I realize that there is nothing wrong with a bit of teenage angst.

It is difficult for me to imagine who I would be if it were not for these characters, as well as so many more. They are as real to me as my friends and parents, and they have all laid bricks in the foundation that has become my personality. This is my favorite part about literature. I may never look out across the Nebraskan plains with Antonia, or attend a party at West Egg with Nick, but in my own mind I already have. I've not only escaped to these far off places and hid with these characters, but I've also found myself. While my love of reading was rooted in forgetting myself, in the process I ended up discovering exactly who I am. I took the pieces that stories offered me, and I put them together in an attempt to craft a smart, independent, compassionate girl, while also recognizing what I didn't want to be. It has been a journey, and I will continue it for the rest of my life as I grow and change with the imaginary people I meet in the pages of my books.

Analysis

Not every essay requires a student to write about their achievements or past successes. Sometimes the best essays just share a student's genuine interest—this is one of those essays. The writer skillfully reveals how the stories they have read have impacted their life in a concrete way, displaying how characters live through them in simple actions like raising their hand in class or standing up against injustice. The underlying themes of social justice ("speak from my heart about injustices I see") and rebellion against gender norms ("greatly outnumbered by my male classmates") also align closely with Swarthmore's culture and demonstrate that the author is a good fit for the school.

The Freedom of Learning
Mina Liang

Each person has one question she would rather not answer - the question she swats away casually, pretending that she had never heard it - and for middle-school Mina, it was the seemingly innocuous question, "What school do you go to?" Blinded by my embarrassment, for many years I could not fathom why my mother, a Ph.D in Economics, would sacrifice the job she loved to become a stay-at-home mom and ostracize her child as a *homeschooler*. Today, I am boundlessly grateful for the real-world perspectives and experiences homeschooling has given me to develop my passions and strong sense of self.

My "normal school day" began when I tramped down the stairs in my pajamas, eager to follow the study plan I had designed for myself. For me, school was simply doing what I loved to do, an extension of my innate curiosities. I would often read for hours about the intricacies of Colosseum architecture, and when I grew tired I would play violin at the Senior Center, listening to my audiences' stories between Mendelssohn movements. Because my "school" had no physical boundaries, I viewed every moment of the day as an opportunity to learn. I studied the art of cooking with my mother, learned to manage resources through my job as a cashier, and practiced my Spanish with friends at ballet class. My animated and inquisitive nature drove my daily routine, and my smooth transition to Deerfield Academy only further amplified the excitement I have with intellectual stimulation.

The individualistic nature of homeschooling for five years, unconventional by many standards, has created my contagiously confident and independent personality. Although I often interacted with others during daily swim practices or visits volunteering at the Senior Center, I was sometimes troubled that I did not have a consistent peer-to-peer social scene. When I first began homeschooling, I found it unsettling not to base my value off of others' opinions, yet it has been this very weaning from dependency on others for approval that has created my internal drive, independent from external pressure from peers and teachers. I listen to Dale Carnegie audiobooks on my drives to school, not to impress my friends, but to seize control of improving my own character. I habitually reflect in my journal, not to receive a 5 on the AP exam, but to internalize the little lessons I have learned throughout the day and commemorate meaningful moments I might otherwise have forgotten. Although I am enthusiastically extroverted, it is during my times of individual reflection when no one else is watching that I find my identity, grounded in a complete sense of self.

With homeschooling freeing me from the burdens of class periods and letter grades, my experiences in the real world working as a cashier revealed to me an acute awareness of my relatively small place within society. Realizing at a young age how school can shield students' eyes from the mundane realities of making a living, homeschooling has created my pragmatic perception that my education is not an end within itself, but a means of preparing for the real world beyond. Homeschooling has given me long-term vision filled with purpose and drive that focuses on how I can utilize my resources to benefit society.

When my mother first sacrificed her career dreams to homeschool me, even my dad and brother dismissed the idea as too risky; today, my mother's success inspires me to unapologetically rely on my own instincts and embrace long-term visions that venture beyond the mainstream of conformity. With my innate curiosity and observational awareness that lead my learning outside of the classroom, homeschooling has given me the confidence and courage to design my own path outside of societal expectations.

Analysis

This essay shows off the student's personality and presents a unique narrative on how their homeschooling background has shaped their development. We see an internal drive for continual self-development ("I listen to Dale Carnegie audiobooks on my drives to school, not to impress my friends, but to seize control of improving my own character") and a clear sense of direction for their academic trajectory ("my pragmatic perception that my education is not an end within itself, but a means of preparing for the real world beyond").

Grocery Store Philosopher
Samantha Ortiz-Clark

I am living a double life.

To the uninformed observer, I am simply an ordinary grocery store checkout girl. I ring up produce, direct people to their desired items, haul bags into carts; all the standard duties of a cashier. It's a simple enough job. Despite only having worked for a few weeks, it's easy for the motions to become automatic: scan, bag, scan, bag. The beauty of the job is in that it is so simple, so mundane, that it goes completely unnoticed, even by the one performing it.

However, in reality, this repetitive motion gives me plenty of time for introspective thought. My secret identity is that of a philosopher.

There's plenty to consider during the eight hour shifts; how the clock seems to creep slowly from one minute to the next like an ant through honey, how I track the crawling minutes as if my very life depended on them, how no other creature in the animal kingdom is bound by the incessant meander of the passing seconds apart from me and my fellow men. I notice how stark the difference is between generations in everything from preferred shopping hours to purchases to payment methods. I wonder whether something is lost in the impersonality of grocery superstores, or whether the lack of variation and individuality for the sake of accessibility and convenience truly does constitute the height of progress.

However, no revelation was quite as profound

as the realization that every single person who walks through the automatic doors is *real*.

The term for it is sonder, and even this name is not official. Sonder, in a legitimate linguistic context, means to probe; however, John Koenig, creator of *The Dictionary of Obscure Sorrows*, coined the term in a contemporary context. Essentially, it is the sudden realization that every single person you interact with, even for the briefest, most insignificant moments, has a life as vibrant, messy, and intricate, as your own.

The man with the face tattoo who comes in at least once a day for junk food and cigarettes has a mother he figures he should call more. The college student who comes through the line with forty frozen burritos and a bottle of plumbing liquid worries about whether he even enjoys the job he works himself to exhaustion for. The old woman with more coupons than purchases struggles with her body image. Even the little boy who scampers up to the counter with just enough change for bubblegum wishes his "friends" were more inclusive.

Every person I greet with the same chirpy catchphrase is as human as I am. They go home to beloved families, they stress over responsibilities, they laugh with their friends, they scream and cry and fall apart over situations they can't change, they put themselves back together in time for work the next morning.

Their roots run as deep as mine, their branches stretch upwards and upwards, just as mine do. They flourish in spring and wither in winter. Tangled vines of grief wind around the trunks of their lives and blossoms of joy open their petals to the sun. My life is more vast and wide than even I can fathom, and I am only one tree in a forest of billions.

It's not so hard to be pleasant to rude customers, or obedient to particularly finicky managers once I remember that they are real people, with real lives and real struggles, just like I am. No one is out to get me; every one is just one person trying to make his or her life the best it can be with what they have. This revelation completely changed both my perspective on others and the way I treat those around me. It helped foster a greater sense of compassion in me. It taught me to be patient and to assume the best of people, because at the end of the day, even the rudest, nastiest people I meet are still just that: *people.*

This epiphany doesn't make me always delighted or endlessly patient. It doesn't automatically make me wake up in the morning thrilled to work a six hour cashier shift every day.

But it certainly gives me something to ponder while I ring up groceries.

Analysis

This is a perfect example of a great essay written about a mundane topic. The student's voice shines through in this essay through their observations and reflections. We learn that they are introspective, mature, and compassionate. We also learn that, despite the monotony of their mundane job, the student exercises thoughtfulness to the best of their ability. The little backstories created for the people in the store ("has a mother he figures he should call more") are clever, humorous, and demonstrate the student's self-awareness. The sentence "This epiphany doesn't make me always delighted or endlessly patient" creates nuance within the essay and shows genuineness instead of neatly wrapping things up in an artificial way. Overall, the entire piece is well-written and gives us a good picture of what this student is like.

On Repentance, Acne, and the Holiest Day of the Jewish Calendar
Zoe Myers-Bochner

Nobody told me
that acne knew
my darkest secrets:

that I would receive
my first pimple
on the end of my nose
at thirteen years old
on Yom Kippur, and spend
a day praying to God,

Is this a sign,
Adonai? Did I so blemish
another
as you now blemish
me?

***

Zits usually reside
on my face
for some time,
but this, the first,
was gone with the fast.

***

On Yom Kippur, my Hebrew school teachers told me, God wrote each person's fate for the next year in the Book of Life. At sunset, God closed the Book, sealing that fate. To be sealed for good required fasting and repentance: sunup to sundown, hungry and parched, on our feet in the sanctuary, atoning for our sins. Yom Kippur wasn't a *holiday* to celebrate, but a *holy day* to be observed.

To the rabbis, Yom Kippur was the holiest day of the year. To other kids at Hebrew School, it was an excuse to skip school for the second time in two weeks. I wondered, what did Yom Kippur mean to me?

At twelve, I became a Bat Mitzvah and formally accepted the responsibilities of a Jewish adult. I'd always believed that I would receive a spiritual revelation on that day, but nothing really changed. I felt two hundred pairs of eyes on mine, numbing my recollection, and then an immense wave of relief.

At thirteen, I received my first-ever pimple on the tip of my nose the night before Yom Kippur. Newly fasting and literally blemished, I felt god was punishing me for something – what, I didn't know – and decided to take stock of myself for the first time.

At fourteen, I decided that I was too quiet and vowed to speak up. At fifteen, I was too outspoken and vowed to listen better. At sixteen, my list of faults was longer than my forearm. At seventeen, I have only seven words: I want to be myself, but better.

Some scoff when I say Yom Kippur is my favorite holiday, for who loves a day of fasting, chest-beating, and standing for hours? Even I used to think that some of the Yom Kippur rituals were pointless: how we starve ourselves every year and promise to change, only to forget our oaths when we break the fast. But Yom Kippur is the one day I have to take stock of myself—to think about the gulf between who I am and who I want to be. The expanse is wide, but looking across that gulf is the first step in building a bridge.

At sundown, I step into the ark. I realize now that there's no literal book of life and my fate for the year is not decided when the sun sets. Still, I feel a sense of grief walking into Shul on the holiest day of the year, grief for the past year and for who I was before...

I listen to the voices around me, and I become lost in them: hundreds of voices united in prayer, each breath forcing out imagined sins, notes and melodies rising to Heaven until they become breathy and crack.

Cracking voices, cracking souls. The old man in the pew behind me sways, eyes closed, as he chants the age-old melody: *Avinu Malkenu*, grant me the courage to move forward. I am grateful for my faith, for a tradition that carves this one day from the mountain of time to simply think: about how far we've come, and how far we have yet to go. That, I think, is something to celebrate.

Analysis

This essay stands out primarily for its contemplative theme and strong sense of maturity. We see that the writer possesses a desire to constantly improve. The student's sentence, "Yom Kippur is the one day I have to take stock of myself—to think about the gulf between who I am and who I want to be," is elegantly put, and demonstrates a high level of self awareness. Overall, this essay in the context of the Jewish tradition gives the reader an insider's look into the writer's growth over the years. It also showcases their personality through an original poem and through their thought processes during each year's Yom Kippur reflection.

QUESTBRIDGE ESSAYS

Reflection on Family Conflict
Anonymous

I drag my feet across the pavement, aware of the dreadful three hours awaiting me. The uproar of the overcrowded parking lot taunts my already morose state of mind. I clench my Harry Potter book tightly upon my chest as I walk through the stained glass doors of the department store. The doors close upon me and I stop myself from shouting "let's leave already!" understanding full well the futility of even attempting to convince my mother.

My teenage sister might as well have been a live mannequin with her splendid outfit. She belongs in the store the moment she steps in. My mother, wearing worn-out jeans and a subtle blouse, looks at me with good-natured humor and tells me to look around, thinking — perhaps hoping — that I will find something I like this time. I attempt to smile and respect her choice of leisure for a few hours. After all, she and my sister leave all their troubles outside those doors as they try on one outfit after another, and I should not rob them of that even though the mall could not be further from my idea of a getaway.

I walk through the mall's doors and I'm pained to see not four, but only three members of my family. Perhaps it is his lingering presence in the store that brings forth the memories I wish to forget. Sadly, my father's departure has driven out what I cherished most in him: his exuberant smile as he came home from a long day at the mechanic's shop, and our trips to the city, where every moment was the best of my ten-year-old life simply because I was with him. The affectionate, devoted father is now a figure I hardly recognize. The man who once gave me piggy-back rides is now the man stagnant on the couch, living on Armenian coffee he asked me to prepare. The man who coaxed me into daily walks to the park now refuses to step outside. The worst part is that he refuses to speak, to tell me why he is acting so... and one day he's just gone. The man I once looked up to is not the man I now remember... and unfortunately, the place of solace for my mother and sister is precisely the place where I recall the drastic change in him.

I look at my mother as she looks upon my sister, and I'm aware of her worries: she must raise her children with clothing on their backs, food on their table, and roof over their heads. Here again the store touches upon my most fragile memories. I look at my mother but I do not see a smiling woman browsing through a rack of clothing—I see an exhausted mother coming home from her night shift at the restaurant, stumbling to her bedroom early in the morning while her children prepare for school. Instead of seeing the vibrant, sky blue dress she is trying on, I see the pale blue of the patient scrubs clinging to her unconscious form after the surgery. I remember her two months of
recovery, riddled with unease as she thinks about finding a job as soon as she is back on her feet.

The three hours at the mall have come and gone. I look at my mother and sister. They are content with their few hours of "peace and quiet" and I could not be happier... "I could not be happier," I repeat over and over to myself, testing it out. "I could not be happier," I repeat another dozen times and realize that this is the truth! I am happy. I am happy because despite being torn away from my beloved Harry Potter, my company is a family that loves me. I am happy because I have the chance to wake up every morning and spend the day with them. I am happy because I know that they will never do what my father has done. They will never abandon me, for they are all too familiar with that lasting and gut-wrenching pain.

We walk out of the store, a family of three, and I know that we have forgiven him. The sleepless nights, the constant arguments between my mother and father, the absence, it is all forgiven... Twelve-year-old me could not understand forgiveness or how strength can arise from difficulties, and honestly, I still do not. Nevertheless, I have forgiven, but I will never forget. I will never forget this lasting bond with my mother and sister, and for that I am thankful.

Analysis

From this essay, we are able to learn about the writer's hardships, and learn a lot about their personality and character along the way.

The introduction does a great job of including details that subtly show what the author is like. We can picture the author sheepishly following their mother and sister with a Harry Potter book. (Tip: Don't be afraid to sprinkle your interests throughout the essay to add some color).

The author also opens up about their hardships, growing up with a single mother who also underwent surgery. Through this, we learn that the author, who likely had to take care of her younger sibling, is resilient, and took on responsibility from a young age.

Lastly, we see that the author cares deeply about family, and is able to find the courage to forgive. This essay's strengths are its storytelling, writing quality, and display of strong character traits.

Discovering STEM
Anonymous

From the opening of the white elliptical container, I could see the bright yellow yoke slushing around. I could see the salt crystals my vocal instructor had sprinkled on the egg whites. I stood there, egg in hand, convincing myself: this is for the best, this will benefit me in the long run, my voice will become softer, the salt will mask the taste. I tipped the egg, felt the slimy contents slide down my throat. The salt did NOT mask the taste. That is when I decided that singing was not for me.

How did I end up in this situation? In a childish bid for attention, I stood in front of my family and sang my heart out, and before I knew it, my mother was encouraging me to seek a professional career in singing. At the age of twelve, my desire for attention was instantly fed during singing lessons. I would stand on stage, sing, and the whole room would applaud. I loved the fabulous trips to various performance locations, and of course I loved the attention that followed suit. I was a budding diva and life was my stage... at least it was for a while.

I soon realized that performing was not simply about talent. I was to suppress my tomboyish fashion sense and dress to impress. My mother dressed me in beautiful clothing (much like what my fashionable sister would wear) before every performance. She fixed my hair, put heels on my feet, make-up on my face, while I kept insisting, "It does not matter how I look. These people have come here to simply hear me sing!" I was too young to understand what audiences want:

beauty along with talent. Really, what audiences want is for people to look as they "should." So, I, a performer, should wear lavish clothing rather than the plain, everyday outfit. I was to change myself, and that was not an option.

As I began high school in the Math and Science Magnet Program, I left the heels and the flamboyant makeup. I transformed myself into a scientist, with my blue Yosemite sweater that served as an armor for my exploration in the math and sciences. I wore the sweater at all times: during math tests, precipitation labs, while growing bacteria. The sweater gave me warmth and confidence, a feeling nonexistent while I stood on the stage and sang.

My newfound fascination for the sciences was the last mark; I told my mother that she could not expect me to be the Armenian poster child. I was no longer going to dress for her pleasure, nor was I going to sing. Knowing full well that something was to be done, I stood up for myself, for what I wished to become, and for who I was.

Analysis

Through this essay, we learn more about the writer's interests and self expression. This author is a singer, but is also a "scientist." Our understanding of this author deepens through all of the details they include about themself, from their "tomboyish fashion sense" to their fascination with science. The last paragraph shows that the author has an independent streak, and is passionate about their interests.

The American Daydream
Patrick Han

"Han Cong! Focus on the lesson!" The shrill command interjected into my daydream as I was exploring my imaginary world, where rules of physics and logic were suspended in ways possible only in the minds of six-year-old boys. It was my first year at my Beijing elementary school, yet this was hardly the first time I had been caught indulging in a private reverie, wrestling with questions for which there seemed no easy answers, from "why is the ocean blue?" to "why do countries fight wars?" I was perpetually asking "why" and "how" and "what if." Because the Communist public school system failed to satisfy my hunger for answers, I dreamed of a place where my imagination could be free from the suffocating shackles of a "learning" method predicated on blind obedience and rote memorization of seemingly meaningless data. Little did I know that my fantasy would soon become a reality.

The following year, my parents made the difficult decision to immigrate to the U.S. in order to offer their children the best education in the world. As an ethnic Korean living in China, I had plenty of experience moving to a country with a distinctly dissimilar culture, but naturally I was terribly nervous, if not petrified, by the prospect of immigrating to a fundamentally disparate society as foreign and unfamiliar as the United States. My callow vision of America was more or less limited to the blurry image of a continent brimming with fast food, movie stars, and blondes speaking in an unintelligible tongue.

Despite my trepidation, I began my first day of school in America armed with the proverb, "Suffering in youth is more valuable than gold." I guess it is a Chinese version of the Nietzschean cliché "That which does not kill us makes us stronger." Whatever fear of alienation and social purgatory I had been fostering was soon dispelled, however, when I met Ms. Duong, the teacher who would change my life. Under her loving and patient tutelage, I fell in love with both the English language and, subsequently, with learning in general. While learning Mandarin as a child entailed tedious memorization, learning English was almost instinctive, and every word was like magic to me. It was at this point when I began to ravenously devour every book I could get my hands on, developing an insatiable hunger for knowledge.

Even more gratifying to me was the emphasis on freedom of thought absent in the authoritarian curricula of China, where teachers did not teach but indoctrinated. Only in an American classroom was a personal opinion safe from censorship and individualism fostered, where teachers taught through dialogue rather than diatribe. I enjoyed my newfound intellectual freedom so much that school became my favorite place to be, a haven where my mind was free to explore the world.

Moving from China to the U.S. paralleled my transition from daily robotic regurgitation to insuppressible infatuation with learning. More importantly, Ms. Duong taught me that the purpose of my education is to enable me to make a positive impact on society by touching the lives of others, as she had mine. I inherited from her a consuming passion for making a tangible difference in the world through my education. That is why I aspire to pursue a career in law. As a lawyer or public interest advocate, I can use my intellect to promote the common good, defend individual rights, and fight for justice, and in doing so, leave this world a better place than I found it. I have yet to find all the answers to the "why" "how" and "what if" questions of my six year old self, but I am enjoying the process and hope to engage in this pursuit all of my life.

Analysis

This essay does a great job of showing readers elements of the author's personality and character. Remember: "the pieces that you can give the admissions officer that pertain to character, personality, drive, and motivation are the *most important, especially if they are written in a relatively interesting way*" (see our chapter on "Essay-writing Advice). This essay is a great example of this.

From the author's childhood daydreams, we learn that the author has been curious and imaginative from a young age. They love asking tough questions and thinking outside of the box. But instead of just saying so, the author demonstrates this by showing the readers the specific questions they asked as a child -- the "whys" and "hows" and "what-ifs" (another great sound bite to help add personality). This adds flavor and makes the intro that much more interesting.

In the next paragraph, the author reveals that they are "an ethnic Korean living in China," with "plenty of experience moving to a country with a distinctly dissimilar culture." From this, we learn that even in youth, the writer has had to endure issues with fitting in and adapt to their surroundings.

In the next paragraph, the author's quoting of a Chinese proverb and "Nietzchean cliche" also add notes of personality, and hint at a sort of intellectual bent (not every high schooler can quote Nietzche). The author goes on to show just how their education in America changed their life— it helped the author blossom into a person who absolutely loves to learn and think freely.

Lastly, this author does a phenomenal job of recounting what they have learned through deep and insightful reflection, and explains how these lessons have shaped their worldview and ambitions (their teacher, Ms. Duong, passed on to them a "consuming passion for making a tangible difference in the world through [their] education," which developed into their desire to pursue law).

All in all, this essay tells a captivating story of a developing and curious young mind, and the content of this essay is able to flow in a style that is unique to the author.

Better or Worse
Patrick Han

I open my eyes to a dark, claustrophobic room populated by the most curious assortment of medical equipment and sharp tools that send chills down my spine. The musty air smells of cleaning solution and mildew. An ominous voice emerges from the darkness. "Better... or worse?" Seeing no choice but to agree to the voice's bizarre game, I let out a hesitant "Better." "I see," replied the voice, oblivious to the irony of the unintended pun. But it did not relent. It asks again, "Better... or worse?"

Heaven knows I would prefer to avoid this whole process altogether if given a choice; I would much rather be finishing Nietzsche's *Thus Spoke Zarathustra*, watching reruns of *Arrested Development*, perusing the Onion, or even flying my kite on this windless day. But alas, I need my eyeglasses to do all of these things, so I sit here patiently while my optometrist interrogates me. Yet this ordeal, as unpleasant as it is, opened my eyes to a profound truth: that achieving clarity in one's vision in life is a long, deliberative process of trial and error. Just as my optometrist methodically tries each lens one by one to find the perfect fit, I too spend my days testing and trying on different visions for my future. And just as she painstakingly grinds the lens uniquely tailored to my vision, I too forge my frame of view using the fragments of knowledge, experience, and ideas I have accumulated in my brief seventeen years of life.

A close friend of mine named Daniel sees me at school the next day and compliments me on my new pair of glasses. "They really bring out the color in your eyes," he jests. It was Career Day, so we blithely amble to class together, looking forward to the relaxed day ahead of us. It was the week before Finals, so we welcomed a short break in the midst of the palpable pressure and stress permeating the halls of Arcadia High School. Our Career Day guest, a restaurant entrepreneur, asks us what kind of professions we plan to pursue after college. When it was Daniel's turn, he spoke without an ounce of hesitation. "Ever since I was in the fifth grade, I knew I would be a kidney surgeon one day."

In fact, the vast majority of my classmates have crystallized a clear, unwavering vision of their professional goals and future endeavors. But not I. I am an outlier in the competitive, career-minded microcosm of Arcadia High School. I have not cemented my goals, not for the lack of aspirations but for the depth of my love of exploring the unknown, of trying new things, of, in the words of Thoreau, living deep and sucking the marrow out of life. I am driven by passions, to be sure, but they are so eclectic that I feel like I am being pulled a million different directions at once. I am propelled by an obsessive desire to try, do, and be everything.

From philosophy and political theory to astrophysics and anthropology, my diverse interests make it difficult for me to pin down a singular path for my intellectual journey. My plans for the future seem to constantly shift, as I plan to become a political scientist one day and an U.N. diplomat the next. At this moment, I happen to be fascinated by law and politics. Law enthuses me because I am captivated by the idea of defending truth and fighting for justice, not with bullets or bombs but with wit and words. I am passionate about politics because it presents real-life solutions to real-life problems. I believe that the purpose of my life is to leave this world a little better than the way I found it, and that the only permanent way to change the world for the better is to change the minds of the people who live in it; both fields allow me to accomplish that.

Despite the wide range of my interests, the overarching theme connecting the seemingly disparate courses and extracurricular activities on my resume is my consuming passion to live life to its fullest and learn as much as I can about the world in order to maximize the difference I can make while I am living in it.

Although my embryonic vision for my future is still a blurry work in progress, the one crystal clear keystone amidst the ambiguous haze is my overarching life goal to make a lasting contribution to humanity in the brief time I have. Trying on each and every worldview I come across, I look at the world around me through different prisms, from iconoclastic or forward-thinking perspectives to their more traditional counterparts. I have yet to find the "Goldilocks" lens that is "just right" for me, but for now, I am content to simply explore the stupendous universe through my inchoate vision and marvel at its perplexing mysteries. Maybe I'll even unlock a few in the process. In any event, I am mindful that, for "better or worse," discovering my own unique vision for my future is going to require a little more time, a lot more thoughtful exploration, and an endless string of introspective questions, many of which tend to be more puzzling than a simple "better... or worse?". Thus I wake up each morning bursting with excitement for the possibilities that lie on the horizon. Although I may be an island of uncertainty in a sea of goal-directed individuals, I eagerly press forward, unsure of what the future may hold but brimming with optimism nonetheless.

Analysis

Elegant and well written, this essay demonstrates the student's intellectual curiosity and wide-ranging interests. Details like "watching reruns of *Arrested Development*, perusing the Onion, or even flying my kite on this windless day" add character and personality to the essay. We see the student's values ("the purpose of my life is to leave this world a little better than the way I found it") and how they plan to live them out ("I am passionate about politics because it presents real-life solutions to real-life problems"). However, the author's reflection that "discovering my own unique vision for my future is going to require a little more time, a lot more thoughtful exploration, and an endless string of introspective questions" is appropriate for a high school senior. This student successfully avoids the mistake of trying to sound perfect. Instead, they are honest about their uncertainty. If you too, are unclear about your specific goals, be careful not to sound like you have no direction in your life. Notice that this author still demonstrates their pursuit of different intellectual interests and highlights what they have learned about the direction they want to go in — "the one crystal clear keystone amidst the ambiguous haze is my overarching life goal to make a lasting contribution to humanity in the brief time I have."

Across the Shelves and Seas
Dalina Nguyen

"Dalina, read book. Novel. History."

Some would raise an eyebrow at that. It almost sounds like a command given to some artificial intelligence. Others would take it as an arbitrary string of words. However, this is the English with which English I grew up, the English to which I was—and still am—exposed.

My parents set foot in the United States in the late 1900s. One traversed the seas; the other the skies. Having immigrated later in life—my mother in her twenties, my father in his thirties—they were not as predisposed to learning the English language. Furthermore, they undertook jobs that required little communication. My mother worked in the textile industry where she was only ever given curt orders, reprimanding scorn, or backhanded approval. My father was employed in technology assembly, again only ever being given mechanical instructions. I suppose it is no wonder they speak to me robotically in English; it is the only way they know how to.

While my sister took ESL, I learnt English from a variety of sources. I absorbed my parents' awkward phrases, cartoon heroes' declarations of war, and most importantly writings concentrated in all sorts of subjects. I was encouraged to read at an early age. My parents believed in establishing my proficiency in English through reading novels, historical nonfiction, and scientific papers. I would be taken to the small public library every week, taking out numerous books at a time. I would be leafing through Burnett's *A Little Princess*, scan-

127

ning Darwin's *On the Origin of Species*, and running my finger across books on the Vietnam War.

As a result, I tended to do better in English classes: teachers placed me in higher-skilled reading groups, my essays were well received and pinned on bulletin boards, and I almost always got perfect scores on my spelling quizzes (you can bet I have yet to spell "occurred" incorrectly since that day in fourth grade). As much as I was enjoying my quality time with "educational" books, as my parents would call them, I felt there was something missing.

That "something" was as simple as reading for entertainment, not for studying syntax. That is not to say I did not find reading about Jupiter's many moons, the life of George Washington, or the tragedy of Romeo and Juliet interesting. Every work had its own element of entertainment. But imagine stumbling across Slim's thrilling, perverse story of *Twilight Eyes* by Dean Koontz. Or Will's adventurous missions in Flanagan's *Ranger's Apprentice* series. Or Alex's torturous times in Furnace Penitentiary.

To my parents' dismay, I began to delve deeper into such electrifying tales. Further fueling my parents' disapproval, I also dipped in my toes to test the waters of Japanese culture. I was fascinated by their otherworldly content and themes. Issues we would never fathom confronting or exposing in our own society, Japan was more than ready to do so. Take *Sailor Moon* for example. Sailors Uranus and Neptune were depicted in a homosexual relationship, although the North American dub censored this. Two strong-willed, powerful lesbians? What more could a chaotically queer teenager ask for?

My parents come from a conservative, traditional background. Essentially, I was raised a homophobe. Of course, that did not go so well. I had already known since preschool that guys were not the only ones who grabbed my attention. I spent my childhood and early teenage years in self-denial, and on the sly, I would rewatch the *Sailor Moon* VHS tapes to admire Uranus and Neptune's relationship. I was envious of how open they were (though it would not be considered as open and revolutionary in today's age). I was frustrated at how normalized Shion and Rat's relationship was in *No. 6* when in real life, the LGBT+ community was ostracized and deemed lunatics.

But gradually, I came to terms with my sexuality. I read books like *Freakboy*, manga like *Irony Dress ni Sayonara*. These works resonated with my struggle of finding my place in the world, my earth-crumbling inner conflict between right and wrong, normal and deviant. They helped me achieve peace with myself. Though presented through different mediums, though created for different audiences, they accomplished the same goal. How?

That is what piqued my interest in comparative literature. I wanted to know how two different literatures could be so distinct yet so similar. How does Huxley's dystopian *Brave New World* compare to that of Tanizaki's gear-shifting *Naomi*? How is it that two societies, separated by such a great distance, have squabbled over the same argument on the purpose of literature? By that, I mean the bad blood between H.G. Wells and Henry James regarding English/American literature and then Junichiro Tanizaki and Akutagawa Ryunosuke regarding Japanese literature.

Maybe telling my parents, "Read book. Novel. History," would inspire a passion within them as well.

Analysis

This essay covers a wide range of topics, from the student's personal development to their scholarly interests. We begin with how reading started as a purely academic pursuit for the student but developed into a medium for self-discovery, helping them find peace with their identity within a hostile community. The student's past experiences inspired their passion for comparative literature, making a convincing argument for their future plan of study.

From 1 to 24/7/365
Dalina Nguyen

I have two whiteboards in my room. One is a calendar, and the other is just your average dry erase notepad.

Nothing about the last two statements sounds groundbreaking, but trust me, my world turned upside down.

Well, actually, it turned right-side up.

Upon entering high school, my mental and emotional state took a turn for the worse. I felt inferior in my academic classes. My elective classes, which were to help me decompress, reduced me to a two-digit figure. The gradual dehumanization high school imposed was overwhelming. I grew to mindlessly output assignments, mechanically take exams, and blindly construct projects. Days blurred together as I would repeat menial tasks purposelessly. I had little motivation to pursue activities outside of school.

Things changed when I got my whiteboard calendar.

I never liked the idea of whiteboards. First and foremost, they reminded me of school, which was not a good idea with me in my condition. Second, I thought of whiteboards as essential tools for sociable, healthy-minded people. I believed that people who had their lives situated owned whiteboards. I associated whiteboards with established, powerful women with hundreds of social events to attend, countless meetings to lead. Under no circumstances was I ready to face the disparity between me and the successful, imaginary woman.

But oh, was I wrong. So very wrong.

Getting a whiteboard allowed me to recognize every day as distinct, separate days. Those two seconds I spent writing the date in the box? They were a full twenty-four hours. And those four centimeters my hand traveled from one square to another? That was an entire day left behind. I was able to visualize all the days I had to start afresh, to start anew. I acknowledged the time I had to cultivate myself, to explore the depths of my interests. I often get told how maniacal I look when I slash through a day with a fat red Expo marker, but I don't think they understand the sensation of knowing the curtains have fallen and that a new act is commencing. No longer did the days blur together in monotony; it was dyed in orange goals and blue meetings. Not quite what a professional's whiteboard would look like, but it's enough for me.

Having only a whiteboard calendar meant there was little space to expand my plans. That is where the second whiteboard comes into play. There, I write quotes to keep pushing onward. Occasionally, I'll doodle a little figure to help drive my motivation. Otherwise, the board is covered in green, pink, and purple categories: to-do, self-growth, and self-maintenance. Schoolwork and critical matters are placed under the to-do list, my hobbies and pursued interests are scribbled under "self-growth," and meditation and self-care techniques are written under "self-maintenance." Not quite as luxurious as flying to Paris for a conference, but I'd rather heal myself through meditation.

Whiteboards are game changers. I may not have an $100,000 income, but I've sure got a priceless lifestyle.

Analysis

A killer opening hooks us from the start. Why does a whiteboard matter so much? In the following paragraphs, we see how the whiteboards are a means of control, helping the student plan and organize their day. We are able to imagine the student as they "slash through a day with a fat red Expo marker" and "write quotes to keep pushing onward." This essay mainly centers around personality, giving the readers a greater sense of how this student thinks and goes about their day. It's a humanizing piece that shows a side of the student we don't see anywhere else in the application.

The Studious Lineage of the Alvarado Family Tree
Cristopher Alvarado

Reminiscing upon the days I spent in Mexico on vacation as a child, there is one memory in particular that sticks out to me: tagging along with my Papá and Abuelito in a wheelbarrow into the tropical forests of Guerrero. Traversing the green orchards of palm trees and prickly vines to pick mangos, I was captivated by the hidden paradise so close to my father's rural hometown. The alleys were unpaved, the houses of rustic concrete construction appeared run down, and yet there was so much liveliness brimming from within the townspeople. Indifferent to the impoverished circumstances, each morning we woke up early in the morning to cut open coconuts or work in the field, smiling and talking incessantly with the blazing sun radiating down upon us. My Abuelito, a loquacious individual, would instill his wisdom in me through anecdotes, reminding me to be studious and to educate myself with the resources my parents provided.

My entire life I've lived with my family in a Spanish-speaking household in a quiet suburban neighborhood, barely out of the reach of the crime infested ghettos prominent in East Charlotte. We never truly associated with our neighbors; our interactions usually consisted of friendly smiles and broken English. Nonetheless, all I needed as a child were my parents. When my father wasn't busy working, we'd spend all of our time together, taking the occasional trip to the $2 movie theater, dining on Whoppers at our local Burger King, or scavenging for treasures on Sunday afternoons after church at the flea market. These tiny excursions fueled my zeal for interaction with people, and in these moments, all that mattered was family.

Two years ago, my Abuelito went missing. Papá was forced to quit his job in order to go to Mexico. Tending to my gravely ill Abuelita and distraught aunts, he kept me and Mamá updated each day he was away.

Confusion. Guilt. Prayer. Rumors. Extortion. Remains.

After the grueling course of a month, my Abuelito was found. Not a single soul heard his last breath.

We couldn't afford to travel and attend the funeral. Following the events of my Abuelito's passing, for half a year we were on food stamps. Our family was supported only by my mother's part time job as a cafeteria lady and my father's lifetime savings. The endless reservoir of optimism I had adopted years ago had begun to run dry. What happened to my paradise, to the carefree residents that seemed to trust one another so freely? How was I supposed to focus on my education when my family's well-being was at risk?

Large textbook full of sticky notes in hand one day, my father told me he had gone to the National Urban League center to study. He was wearing the same face of determination when I came home from school. Papá intended to continue being the provider of the household. I then realized how naive it was to think that the only motivation for my academic success was my family's pride. I couldn't sulk about the present when I had the pieces in front of me to shape a bright future. I had to challenge my fears the very same way my father did. I made a solemn oath that I would use my education to provide for my parents long into their old age.

This experience was followed by my most difficult decision: leaving home. Almost a year after my father had received his certificate from the Urban League, my undivided attention to academics bore fruit to success. I had been accepted into the NC School of Science and Mathematics. This was the opportunity I had been awaiting to truly make an impact; to start anew as my father had done.

I soon realized that my family's presence in my life and the roots of Hispanic identity they had cultivated within me were the key to my success. The joyful townspeople in Mexico, my grandfather's stories, and my father's determination have all been lovingly gifted to me. I have learned from their example, been inspired by their love, and know that I must not waste these important lessons that they have striven so earnestly to impart to me. My greatest strength had always been listening to others, but now I'm able to tell my own stories and help others share their own. For an entire year I've aimed to build a community of never-ending smiles and laughter, safe from harm. I've learned how valuable simply having a conversation with someone else is for building a community and achieving opportunities. This is how I remember my Abuelito: by embracing those who have blessed me with strength and lending a hand to those who need mine with a picture, a song, or a simple, sincere smile.

Analysis

Vivid imagery and a compelling story help this essay stand out. We get a solid sense of the student's background and what drives their intense educational focus. Lessons of strength, family, and love are interwoven into this essay, presenting a raw and honest look into the student's life. This essay is a great example of what an authentic voice sounds like—- one of the key elements of a great essay that is so difficult to capture.

100 Instrumentals, 1 Perfect Song
Cristopher Alvarado

On weekend late nights I'm often lost in deep introspection, headphones isolating me from my environment. I envision the poetry in my head set aflame, rekindling an entire week's worth of emotion as a snapshot of my life. One week, it's the pounding heart and rush of adrenaline from trying to keep up with my teammates during rugby practice. The next, it's the sigh of relief and satisfaction after getting an A on a month-long computer project. To me, the epitome of artistry is the release of imaginative expression. It's during the moments spent producing music on my laptop that I let go of my inhibitions of being judged by others and begin whispering life into the melodious scenery.

Over the last four years, I've spent countless hours making nearly one hundred electronically produced songs. As a novelty seeker, I love composing because of the endless variation, hundreds of sounds and samples available to my disposal. They reflect the culture of millions of people. What made them sing praise like I do at Mass, cry with anguish after a loved one's passing, or shout for revolution against discrimination? They meld noise into sweet melodies of our human consciousness.

I've written lyrics for very few songs during the same four years. When passion strikes a chord within me, I put down my thoughts on paper. Nostalgia for my family hit last year after being away from my parents at boarding school for so long. I like to interpret my ode to them, written in Spanish, as a salute to the Latinos who struggle to find their own voice, who cannot figure out what path lies ahead in their life. However, at heart, it is a pure love song. Romantics like me ambitiously search for the ideal subtleties in human character.

My song, "Sigo Sin Encontrarte," reached my family in Mexico through Facebook days after I composed it. They could see me for the first time in almost three years in the form of music. Hundreds of miles away, my 9-year-old niece Melanie was listening to it every day, dancing and giggling to her new favorite song. This was the power of sharing a message and it could not have meant more from anyone else. The infectious rhythm and the tropical vibes of the song call out to others to dance with me and celebrate the music around us.

I dream of a life in which I can produce music for anyone, as a hobby or a profession. Organizing karaoke nights for my entire hall, playing with friends in the French Horn section of the wind ensemble, and hiding tidbits of my music in all of my video projects are all evidence of this dream. I've worked tirelessly, taking audio production and music theory classes to improve upon my abilities and effectively start and lead an audio production club next trimester. The musical canvas at school is never-ending. When the community subconsciously starts humming my music, I'll know I've made my mark.

Analysis

This essay is beautifully written, and excels at showing readers what the author's interests and talents are. Even in the intro, readers catch a glimpse of a wide variety of interests, from rugby to computer science. Additionally, the writer shows deep thought in their meditations on culture, artistry, and self-expression. Readers learn that this person is a romantic. Readers also see that this person is totally absorbed in their passion for music, having written dozens of songs. The author is driven and hard-working, as shown in their tireless work, "taking audio production and music theory classes." In the last paragraph, the author explains their lofty dreams and plans to share their music with everyone. The admissions office can be confident that this person will enrich the campus community with their deep interest in music and love for spreading that interest.

WHY SWARTHMORE
ESSAYS

Suleyman Amjad

There are multiple reasons why I see myself at Swarthmore College. First, Swarthmore provides a unique environment that focuses on collaboration rather than on competition. It's clear from my conversations with Swarthmore alumni, that while Swarthmore is an academically challenging environment, the culture allows students to strengthen critical thinking skills and develop the ability to work in a team at the same time. Whether it was building remote control planes with my friends or trading solos in a Jazz combo, working together heightened the learning experience for me, and I believe this is what I will find at Swarthmore.

Swarthmore students believe in influencing the world in a real way and that is inspiring to me. Community service and involvement are important parts of my life, and I see myself continuing the Swarthmore tradition to improve the lives of others. Using the skills gained from my classes to help tutor students in rural Ghana was an incredibly rewarding experience, and I know that this mentality is a core part of life at Swarthmore.

Swarthmore's well-rounded curriculum will also help me connect my passions of writing and engineering to support my career goal to practice Intellectual Property Law. Swarthmore's General Engineering program will give me a broad technical background and give me a foundation for law school after attending Swarthmore.

In summary, I sincerely believe that encouraging intellectual curiosity and passion for broad based learning are the foremost goals of a Swarthmore education, which resonates with my background and ambitions.

Analysis

This essay is strong because of its structure and specific reasons for choosing Swarthmore. A reader can easily pinpoint the three or four specific reasons why Swarthmore stands out to the author: 1) collaborative environment, 2) community engagement, 3) academic offerings, and 4) broad-based learning. Although their writing on each point is short, they are able to convincingly back up each point with past experience. Their anecdotes about experience building planes and trading solos *shows* that collaboration has played a big role in their life, and that it is important to them. Their experience tutoring students in rural Ghana is unique, and fits in perfectly with Swarthmore's commitment to public service. Their interests in Intellectual Property Law and Engineering, two seemingly disparate fields, and their simultaneous love for writing and engineering are a great match for the complete liberal arts education that Swarthmore offers. They also show diverse, well-rounded interests throughout the essay. Overall, this essay contains concrete, compelling reasons why this person would thrive at Swarthmore.

Chrisbet Cortes-Lopez

The beautiful fall colors and sprawling campus was my first impression of Swarthmore. As I dug deeper I discovered many amazing opportunities unique to Swarthmore, like the Lang Center. In particular, I am deeply interested in the Urban Inequality and Incarceration initiative, as it strongly aligns with a passion I uncovered in high school for criminal injustice. My Sociology of Law class sophomore year, inspired me to read texts like Bryan Stevenson's "Just Mercy: A Story of Justice and Redemption" and Michelle Alexander's "The New Jim Crow: Mass Incarceration in the Age of Colorblindness," which led me to intern with a juvenile justice commissioner. Through projects like the Inside-Out Prison Exchange, UII would allow me to continue learning about these relevant issues while actively making connections in the surrounding Swarthmore area. The opportunity to participate in this work would be an ideal introduction to a career addressing the disproportionate incarceration of people of color through research and advocating for change-- something UII is already doing with after school youth programs and researching impacts of incarceration on children who have an incarcerated parent.

The UII initiative coursework appeals to me academically because it combines so many topics that I'm interested in like psychology, political science, and ethnic studies. With Swarthmore's unique opportunity to create my own major, I plan to design a major that combines each of these interest areas. Learning about these issues through a psychological perspective will allow me to see the cognitive, social, and developmental aspects

of a person's behavior. Learning how the criminal justice system works on a societal level will better help me
see the big picture. Lastly, working with families and
communities through programs like UII will reveal how,
using all of this knowledge and experience, I can one day
make an impact.

Analysis

This person chose to go deep with one main
theme, instead of covering many different reasons. They
are able to do this effectively by including concrete details.

The first paragraph is strong because it clearly
shows why the author is interested in criminal justice,
and why UII matches their interests perfectly. In particular, these two sentences are excellent: "The opportunity
to participate in this work would be an ideal introduction to a career addressing the disproportionate incarceration of people of color through research and advocating for change-- something UII is already doing with
after school youth programs and researching impacts
of incarceration on children who have an incarcerated
parent." They show that the student wants to pursue a
career "addressing the disproportionate incarceration of
people of color," and they support this claim by mentioning past experiences. They also describe how UII is
the perfect continuation of these past experiences, specifically because of the research and action components
of the program (Inside-Out Prison Exchange and after
school youth programs). This person has clearly looked
into UII quite a bit, and has clearly defined reasons behind their plans. A reader can't help but feel that the

student's ambitions and past experiences are a perfect match for UII.

However, this essay is also not one-dimensional. The author shows that they exemplify the liberal arts ethos of having diverse interests. They have clearly done their research about Swarthmore by discussing their plan to unite these interests under a special major (something that not many colleges or universities do). The effectiveness of this essay lies in their ability to (1) *explain* something specific about their interests (criminal justice, psychology, political science, and ethnic studies) and (2) mention something specific about Swarthmore (UII, special major) that meets those needs.

Haron Kalii

I first encountered Computer Science in ninth grade. Soon after, I found love in Databases, and an intellectual pursuit was born. Two years later, over the course of one grueling week, I developed a library database that catalogued the thousands of books in our school. At Swarthmore, I can advance my understanding of databases through classes like CS44 and learn solutions for efficiency and scalability in database systems. I can also reach out to a Computer Science Ninja when I need a helping hand.

Additionally, I can explore diverse courses without worrying about grades in my first semester, thanks to the pass-fail system. Coming from a community that values specialization and quiet compliance, my many interests have often been shunned. However, being at Swarthmore ensures that I'm not forced to discreetly play my music in sugarcane fields at midnight, or read my romantic poetry to maize plants. From learning music composition from Professor Gerald Levinson, to exploring poetics under Professor Nathalie Anderson, Swarthmore opens up a new world where I need not be intimidated by my once furtive intellectual curiosities.

I can also continue to wed my academic interests to community service. Engaging in my community, whether back in Kenya or at Swarthmore, is important to me. In August, I pioneered a seminar for students in my community to emphasize the importance of education. In the same vein, I look forward to tutoring and also mentoring children at Chester through the "Dare 2 Soar" program.

Analysis

This essay is strong because it talks about the author's past experiences, and how they relate to what they want to pursue at Swarthmore. The author loved databases and developed a library database in high school, and wants to continue learning about databases at Swarthmore. The author had to specialize in Kenya, so they love that Swarthmore encourages exploration of diverse interests. They also conducted education seminars as a way to give back to their community, and they want to continue this work through Dare 2 Soar at Swarthmore. Notice this essay's structure. The author focuses on three specific buckets -- computer science, opportunities to explore diverse interests, and community service. For each of them, the author 1) concisely describes their relevant prior experiences and 2) mentions one or two *specific* activities through which they will continue down these paths at Swarthmore. This makes for a compelling essay, because it *shows* the reader your commitment to your interests and explains to admissions officers why Swarthmore is the ideal next step in your trajectory.

Takeaways:
1)   Write a targeted, structured essay. Highlight two or three buckets of things you like about Swarthmore, instead of writing a scattered laundry list of plans.
2)   Make sure to back up your plans at Swarthmore with reasoning, sources of inspiration, or examples

of things you did in the past.

3)   Name two specific opportunities that you want to take advantage of for each bucket. Avoid being vague.

Anonymous

My first glimpse of Swarthmore revealed its energetic and vibrant campus, as Swatties engaged in an intense snowball fight and sledded down a snow-covered Parrish Beach. Searching for the epigenetics classroom, I encountered a student who, coincidentally, was headed to the same class. My impromptu tour guide revealed that this class was her favorite, despite the intensity of the coursework. I could see why, as I observed students excitedly pose questions about their homework readings, encouraging their classmates to think about the head-scratching implications of the papers. After class, Dr. Vecsey approached me to further explain polyphenisms and eusociality. Students and professors took time to discuss their interests because at Swarthmore, ideas are worth sharing. I am drawn to Swarthmore because unlike students who wonder why they have to take a humanities class even though science is their passion, I learn for the thrill of a new idea or the wisdom of a broadened perspective, and I quickly realized that Swatties share this sentiment. I could easily imagine sharing research findings with a friend on a walk through Crum Woods, or spreading scientific awareness through the *Swarthmore Journal of Science*. (Fashioning a foam sword to withstand the annual Pterodactyl Hunt would also certainly make my to-do list.) At Swarthmore, I would continue to explore and cultivate my curiosities; embraced by a community of brilliant, passionate and open-minded individuals, I would be continually inspired to apply all that I am, and excited to discover whom I will become.

Analysis

The strength of this essay lies in the author's ability to convey their love for Swarthmore's liberal arts culture. The student loves being surrounded by peers who are intellectually curious, and genuinely in love with their classes. They show that they love to learn for the sake of learning.

They are also able to help the admissions officer imagine them at Swarthmore. Their love for Swarthmore and reasons for their interest are more general, but they are able to still be specific by showing admissions officers concrete activities they would love to engage in, like walking in Crum Woods, writing for the *Swarthmore Journal of Science*, or participating in the Pterodactyl Hunt.

Megan Wu

While visiting Swarthmore and listening to J.T. Duck speak about the Honors program, I envisioned my senior thesis reviewed by the world's foremost philosophers, flown in from across the country—it would be incredible to have my ideas challenged and legitimized by those whose peer I hope to eventually become. At Swarthmore, I will continue to fight for women's seats at the table by reviving the Lady Philosophers discussion group, perpetuating Swarthmore's female academic heritage. After all, Carol Gilligan, whose writing catalyzed my research in and passion for deliberative democracy, was a Swarthmore alumna. Swarthmore's philosophy faculty specialize in areas from aesthetics to math—for every interest I will undoubtedly have, there is someone who can answer my questions and inspire fifty more. I look forward to revising Kant with philosophy Professor Krista Thomason to show that normative theories are proactively inclusive of marginalized perspectives. Though I hope to pursue a philosophy PhD, the value of challenging myself outside the field is compelling. Swarthmore offers the rare advantage of the pass/fail semester, when I can explore academic fields like multivariable calculus and organic chemistry, classes that aren't offered at my high school. While the experience of being an independent debater was transformative, I always longed for a tightly-knit, collaborative debate team. It would be an honor to represent the Peaslee Debate Society and have the chance to follow in the footsteps of Miriam Pierson (my favorite debater to watch!) by adding to Swarthmore's legacy of phenomenal female debate talent.

Analysis

This essay is powerful because of the specific and concrete reasons that the student has for choosing Swarthmore. Details like "I look forward to revising Kant with philosophy Professor Krista Thomason to show that normative theories are proactively inclusive of marginalized perspectives" demonstrate that the student has actively engaged with the topics she's interested in (i.e., they didn't just search up "Kant" on Wikipedia and insert it into this essay; they've actually studied and read philosophy) and has done the research to pinpoint what Swarthmore can do to advance those interests. The student also brings up an important aspect of Swarthmore —- intellectual community. When the student writes "it would be incredible to have my ideas challenged and legitimized by those whose peer I hope to eventually become," we see that the student is coming to Swarthmore to actively participate in the intellectual exchange of ideas and is open-minded enough to entertain different viewpoints. The student also provides concrete past experiences to show the reason why they plan on participating in the activities they say they will at Swarthmore ("reviving the Lady Philosophers discussion group... whose writing catalyzed my research in and passion for deliberative democracy").

Anonymous

My third culture upbringing in Japan, the United States, and Singapore have brought me the privileges of participating in different educational systems: Montessori, International Baccalaureate, and both Japanese and American public school systems. These experiences have revealed to me an important role of education: building positive relationships across cultural and social differences. This has sparked my interest in improving how we educate young people and how we prepare them to overcome differences in perspectives in order to achieve success in our rapidly changing world.

Swarthmore will help me refine the perspectives and skills to pursue my goals in advancing education. Through the Educational Studies program, I will design a multidisciplinary curriculum focused on providing me innovative approaches to observing and analyzing education. To guide me through this unique curriculum, I will seek the guidance of Swarthmore mentors. I hope to study under Professor Jennifer Bradley because her work in comparing teaching practices in both China and the United States can guide my passion for understanding how culture can transform educational strategies and outcomes in different societies.

In addition, Swarthmore can offer me numerous opportunities to work with others in making a positive impact for young people. I am interested in Swarthmore's partnerships with outside organizations so that I can apply the learnings from my educational studies in meaningful projects. At Swarthmore, I will work with the College Access Center of Delaware County in guiding high school students in the process of applying to universities and identifying future academic goals.

Analysis

This essay is terrific because it leverages the student's unique international background but frames it in a very specific way— different educational systems. While many students write essays discussing their multicultural identity, those essays are typically vague and say something along the lines of "because of my exposure to various cultures, I learned to empathize with people from different backgrounds." This essay does nothing of the sort.

Instead, this student presents a convincing argument that their wide-ranging academic experiences sparked their interest in the educational studies program at Swarthmore. They go into detail on how Swarthmore will help them "refine the perspectives and skills to pursue my goals in advancing education," and name a specific professor they would like to work with. The closing paragraph reflects Swarthmore's social impact ethos and establishes this student as a person who will take initiative to improve their local community in a way that aligns with their personal and academic interests ("I will work with the College Access Center of Delaware County in guiding high school students in the process of applying to universities and identifying future academic goals").

Skylar Thoma

When I began my college search, Swarthmore was yet another small, prestigious liberal arts college near a big city, at which I could satisfy my academic passion and be prepared for the real world (*snore*). Of course, Swarthmore isn't quite as generic as that: its honors program rivals Ph.D programs at graduate schools. I greatly admire Swarthmore for promoting academic collaboration, and admire it even more after Swarthmore scrapped its football program to accommodate students with other talents and passions.

However, as mentioned earlier, Swarthmore is one of many colleges that have quality academic programs. My decision to attend a college has to be based on more than that: can I see myself living there? I got an inkling of that answer when I saw the promotional materials: no other college has the audacity to include conversational flow charts which include the phrase "*tap dances*". I immediately wanted to experience Swarthmore's unique personality first-hand.

When I visited campus last spring, I found that campus life was just like the promotional materials: an eccentric blend of academics and personal passions. I could see myself living the life of the typical Swarthmore geek: exploring political theory in perfectly-sized classes, having fun with Screw Your Roommate, and debating campus politics with my peers. Swarthmore isn't just a place to learn -- it is an opportunity to act on my passions, while surrounded by the quirkiest nerds in the country. That is everything I could ask for.

Analysis

This essay does a great job of playing to its audience.

The introduction is sure to give admissions officers a kick. For many students, their reasons for applying to Swarthmore are nothing more than what the author writes in the first sentence. The essay stands out, because it indicates that the reasons for the student's interest in Swarthmore are much deeper than that. The author also gets extra brownie points for knowing a relatively obscure fact about Swarthmore scrapping its football team.

The author also uses Admissions' unique outreach emails as a vehicle to show that Swarthmore's unique personality resonates with him. An admissions officer's reaction to the second paragraph would surely be, "Yes! The type of student who loves '*tap dances*' is exactly the type of person we want to apply to Swarthmore." The student also shows that they are asking the right questions and thinking deeply about their college application choices when he says, "My decision to attend a college has to be based on more than that: can I see myself living there?" An admissions committee would applaud, and think, "Exactly!" In this essay, you should aim to put yourself and the admissions officer on the same page, by showing that you've done your research on Swarthmore and thought carefully through your decision.

All in all, the author does a great job because they are able to weave many specific details about Swarthmore (e.g. its honors program essentially being a baby Ph.D) into an essay whose voice conveys the spirit of Swarthmore and is just plain fun for admissions officers to read. It is self aware and smartly written. It conveys strong thinking skills and a sense of purpose and direction. By the end of the essay, admission officers will be echoing the last sentence, thinking, "What else can we ask for?"

Yin Xiao

When I briefly visited Swarthmore, I was astonished by its environment – a perfect combination of humans and nature. After researching online, I discovered that Swarthmore's strong sense of community, intellectual excellence and commitment to social justice resonate with me.

As a boarding student, I understand the opportunities in a close-knit community to learn about different cultures. As head of International Club, I realise how cultural gaps can lead to misunderstanding between students and conflicts between nations. As a Chinese student living in Canada, I have been through this adjustment process, and at Swarthmore, I would like to continue to serve as a bridge between cultures by participating in clubs such as *I-20 International Club* and *Multi* to create a community in which interconnection between students can be explored.

While Swarthmore's sense of community appeals to me, I'm also drawn to Swarthmore's rigorous academics. The small seminars will allow me to engage in intellectual debates and bring my experience with different cultures, adding unique dimensions to the conversations.

Community service is as important to me as academics. Though my experience tutoring inner city children, I understand the responsibility of students from privileged academic opportunities to serve those less fortunate. At Swarthmore I see myself participating in programs such as *Lang Scholar* and *community based learning* to "shape a more just and compassionate world."

My visit to Swarthmore gave me a glimpse into the possibilities available. Now I want to take full advantage of the opportunities and immerse myself in this community.

Analysis

This student presents several concrete reasons for choosing Swarthmore and heavily emphasizes the *community* aspect that is core to a small liberal arts college of 1,600 students. The first paragraph presents a thesis of sorts ("I discovered that Swarthmore's strong sense of community, intellectual excellence and commitment to social justice resonate with me") that lays the roadmap for the remainder of the essay. This essay hits on all the big points such as engaging with different communities, rigorous academics, and giving back to those who are less privileged. While somewhat formulaic, the structured approach of this essay reliably gets the job done.

Sam Shih

I am drawn to Swarthmore's dedication to a multi-dimensional experience across academics and extra-curriculars. I plan to major in Computer Science, but look forward to expanding my intellectual foundation in complementary areas such as linguistics and social science. In particular, Swarthmore's classroom ratio of eight students to one professor would give me the support I need to deepen my academic experience, and maybe even design my own major to integrate all my interests. Swarthmore would allow me to study abroad, hopefully in Nepal, and expand my cultural awareness while exploring computer science from a different vantage point. Also, the project-oriented explorations in Swarthmore's SPEED program are a perfect fit for my desire to apply computer science to a variety of fields and will provide me with an unparalleled preparation for real-world professions that require interdisciplinary solutions.

Finally, Swarthmore's roots in civic and social responsibility hits home for me. Self-fulfillment isn't just about profiting from the newest tech in the Silicon Valley bubble, but also about addressing the social issues around us. After feeling the satisfaction of raising over $12,000 for the Typhoon Haiyan victims in the Philippines, I believe that a technical education supported by active involvement in Swarthmore's socially aware student culture can help me achieve my dream of utilizing technology to said humanitarian relief work all around the world.

Analysis

This essay is tightly focused on the student's interest in computer science and technology. However, a key part of this essay that warrants emulation is its effective demonstration of why the student wants to choose Swarthmore to further their computer science education. Arguably, there are many other "tech powerhouse" schools that might be better suited for a student interested in computer science, but this students writes that they want to "expand[ing] my intellectual foundation in complementary areas" and "design my own major to integrate all my interests" which shows that they've thought deeply about why Swarthmore is the best place for them.

An excellent *Why Swarthmore* essay goes beyond why you want to go to Swarthmore; it shows that there are specific traits *unique to Swarthmore* that appeal to you, even though there are a number of other elite colleges and universities that are also exceptionally well-suited for your interests (e.g., why wouldn't a person who is passionate about tech go to MIT or UC Berkeley instead?). You must convey that Swarthmore *in particular* is the school for you, for this essay to be convincing. This is what this essay does well. Finally, the closing paragraph on civic and social responsibility ties in this student's previous humanitarian work and desire to continue advancing it at Swarthmore.

Sandy Shen

Instead of suffocating in a crowded, noxious cafeteria, I prefer to spend my lunches playing my viola or reviewing class material in the tranquility of my school orchestra room. In fact, it was during one of these afternoon practices that I first heard about Swarthmore. My orchestra teacher had handed me a flyer, telling me to "check out their private lesson program." So after researching more about the Music 48 program and talking to alumni, it didn't take long for me to see myself right at home in Swarthmore's small, warm classes, embracing my heritage in Chinese Calligraphy or analyzing healthcare regulation under the guidance of Professor Magenheim. Even more importantly, I knew I would be able to find a comfortable balance between learning, playing the viola, advocating for UNICEF, and potentially serving on the Student Health Advisory Council.

But Swarthmore's emphasis on passionate, dedicated educators is truly its most attractive characteristic. Every memorable experience I have had -- whether revising a draft for the hundredth time or passing an orchestral audition -- has been influenced by the peers I worked with and the mentors I looked up to. I know that the time I spend at Swarthmore will be full of enriching experiences where I can combine all of my passions -- musical, political, academic -- and share them with other people who love what they do.

Analysis

This essay is tight and dense, and it efficiently and eloquently shows admissions officers what exactly spoke to the author of this essay when they researched

Swarthmore -- opportunities to pursue diverse interests and great teachers. They love Swarthmore's small classes and awesome class selection (calligraphy? Healthcare regulation? Come on). The fact that this person wants to pursue "learning, playing the viola, advocating for UNICEF, and potentially serving on the Student Health Advisory Council" also shows their diverse interests and inner drive.

This essay also takes up only 224 words out of the 250 word limit. It is okay not to fill out every single word if you feel that you've said everything you need to.

Yangchen Lhamo

Sweet Swarthmore, I'm going to bow down on one knee and serenade you on why you're awesome, on why I'm awesome, and why we, like Taylor Swift, belong together:

You're one of a kind,
Always on my mind,
One of your founders is Lucretia Mott,
so I already respect you a lot
You're really inclusive and diverse
WIth a rigorous liberal arts education that I want to immerse
in. You're also really LGBTQ friendly
Had cool sidewalk chalk that said "My homosexual relationship is not for hetero consumption"

I like the values you teach your students
Mission statement is to develop ethical and social concern
That's what I want to learn
I love your close-knit collaborative community and building meaningful relationships with my professors, I'm a fan.
I also love interdisciplinary studies and having the chance to design my own major
Gonna combine sociology, economics, and political science- that's major
I believe I can follow all my passions in you
like doing independent social science research to expand my worldview
I'm all about social justice and intersectionality
Want to contribute to your publication, VISIBILITY

Zine, on marginality

A hottie that wants to be a Swattie
I'm gon study human relations and surpass your expect-
ations
If you don't hit me with that congratulation,
Imma pretend we never had this conversation
MC Yang peace out

Analysis

Risky and quirky to the highest degree, we don't recom-
mend that most students do something like this. The
truth is admissions officers have seen countless essays
that are poems, raps, etc. and doing something like this
isn't as unique as you think it might be. However, if you
do feel so compelled, doing something like this might be
a great way to showcase your personality. The strength
of this essay lies more in that it has strong fundamen-
tals for the student's reasons for choosing Swarthmore—
reasons like acceptance of LGBTQ+ individuals, interdisciplinary studies, and social justice activism.

Mina Liang

Growing up listening to my brother share his stories at Swarthmore, as a young girl I impatiently waited for the day that I could experience Swarthmore's intimate seminars, tight-knit swim family, and passionate student body for myself.

My background in homeschooling and Deerfield Academy renders Swarthmore's highly individualized and rigorous learning environment perfect for my learning style. Embracing Swarthmore's 8:1 faculty ratio and small classroom setting, I look forward to the personal connections and discussions I can share with my peers and professors. With 30% of students eventually pursuing doctoral programs attesting to Swat's cultural focus on academia, I would love to experience the Honors Program which would surround me with driven peers and well-respected scholars: the epitome of interactive learning.

With my wide array of extracurricular passions, I look forward to Swarthmore's rich community life beyond the classroom. I am excited to network and connect with other Swatties interested in business through Refine Her Street. To continue my past four years of Chamber Music studies, I look forward to collaborating with Swarthmore's musicians through the Fetter Chamber Music Program. Above all, I am excited to follow my brother's legacy in being a part of the Swat Swim family. Through our conversations, I want to swim under a coach as personable and visionary as Coach Colby.

I look forward to joining Swarthmore's artistic, athletic, and academic communities as another Liang proud to represent the Garnet!

Analysis

This essay is very complete and well-structured. Most of her content falls into two buckets -- learning environment, and activities. She shows that she has done her research, and it is clear that she loves Swarthmore's tight-knit community and rigorous academics (Honors). Admissions officers can also be confident that the author will contribute to Swarthmore's campus in the way of involvement in a myriad of activities.

Jacinta Fernandez-Brough

I have always been called somewhat argumentative, whether discussing the value of religion, the logic behind gun ownership, or the name soccer or football (football naturally) – I relish the thrill of respectful disagreement. As my vocabulary has developed I now refer to my passion as 'constructive debate' and for this reason Swarthmore instantly appealed to me.

From the myriad American colleges the distinctive allure of Swarthmore's unique Honours Program, based on the Oxford tutorial system, has drawn me in. I have found debating legal issues at Moot Court and resolutions at Model United Nations to be engaging activities. Looking towards college I feel a programme centered on a three hour weekly seminar, which emphasises free-flowing discussion, to be an effective form of education well suited to my learning style.

Scholarship with real world application appeals to me, and while visiting Swarthmore I was interested to learn of the external expert examiners of the Honours Programme and practical student projects such as solar powered scoreboards. I discovered an academic environment strongly focused on the application of knowledge that I am looking for in my college education.

Having grown up in an international community, I was also attracted by the opportunities at Swarthmore to study in a range of environments - with semesters abroad, domestic exchange programmes, and externships. In the next chapter of my education I hope to be challenged by stimulating debate in a variety of settings, which I believe I would find at Swarthmore.

Analysis

This essay highlights the student's desire for intellectual debate and argumentation. We see their background in Moot Court and Model UN, and the parallel with Swarthmore's honors program convinces us that they will take advantage of this unique program that Swarthmore provides. The focus on practical application of one's education in the second to last paragraph shows us that this student aims to make a difference.

William Han

When I first visited Swarthmore, I thought to myself, "tiny school for nerds." Not for me. But over the next four years, as my brother Patrick described his experiences, I began to fall in love with Swarthmore's unique personality.

Swarthmore, I learned, was a place where I can be surrounded by people who are as passionate as I am about learning for the sake of learning. A place where I can learn from professors who not only are leaders in their fields, but genuinely love teaching curious minds. A place where students work together in a collaborative environment, without class rankings. All this stands in contrast to my competitive high school, where classes are hated, few care about self-development, and the ultimate purpose of school, for teachers and students alike, is a bigger paycheck. In light of its focus on intellectual curiosity, Swarthmore sounds like paradise. At Swarthmore, I will also grow as an entrepreneur by majoring in economics and participating in programs like the SwatTank business competition and the LAX conference. From Swarthmore's liberal arts approach, I will learn to apply thinking frameworks from other fields to business, just as Steve Jobs combined technology with the humanities. Liberal arts will also teach me to engineer solutions by questioning assumptions and conventions, a critical thinking method Elon Musk calls "thinking from first principles."

After seeing what Swarthmore really stands for, I've discovered that my intense love for learning is in fact a perfect match for this "tiny school for nerds."

Analysis (by Sean Cheng)

This essay effectively incorporates both humor and a strong understanding of what Swarthmore can offer to present a strong case of why this student would thrive at Swarthmore. By mentioning specific extra-curriculars like SwatTank and the LAX conference, the student conveys a desire to apply their learning beyond the classroom and bring a liberal arts mindset towards fields like business and entrepreneurship. The student goes from observing that Swarthmore is a "tiny school for nerds" that was "not for [him]" to discovering that it "is in fact a perfect match," demonstrating that they've thought deeply about why they want to attend Swarthmore. Comparing their high school experience to what they hope college will be like further solidifies these claims that this student specifically chose Swarthmore for its supportive environment and intellectual community.

Anonymous

Sitting on the field, I looked around; why did none of my teammates look like me? Curious about this phenomenon, I conducted a research project interviewing my Asian American teammates to document their experiences within soccer. The work of Dr. Michael Mullan, and his course, "The Tribal Identity of Sport: Nationalism, Ethnicity, and the Rise of Sport in the Modern Era," explore questions like this. In it, students learn how sports help create a collective group identity, an effect my Asian American teammates did not feel, as they were marginalized in sports because of their race. Dr. Mullan's research explores the history of sports within the Japanese American experience, and I would love to extend his work further in understanding the modern function of sports in shifting public perceptions around race and the assimilation of people of color in predominantly white spaces.

The Lang Center for Civic and Social Responsibility emphasizes creating social change through education with the faculty-led initiatives that connect coursework to projects. While visiting Swarthmore, I witnessed this commitment to community-oriented learning through the Inside-Out Prison Exchange project. Students applied their knowledge and developed a manual helping inmates with appeal cases while suggesting reform for Pennsylvania public defenders. Already interested in prison reform from my involvement with Mock Trial and the Innocence Project, I am eager to leverage my education to improve the communities around me. I know that at Swarthmore, serving others will always be a priority.

Analysis

If you've read other essays in this book, you'll notice that many essays love to talk about Swarthmore's 8:1 student to faculty ratio, or its one-of-a-kind honors program. While these are great reasons for wanting to go to Swarthmore, oftentimes a deep dive into specific reasons is more effective (see essay #2 for another example). This essay does a really great job of roadmapping the author's interest in the Asian American athletic experience, and clearly shows how Swarthmore is the perfect place to continue pursuing that interest, under the tutelage of Dr. Mullan. The author expresses a strong commitment to civic engagement -- something that Swarthmore admissions pays attention to (see Essay-writing Advice Chapter under Key Essay Qualities for Liberal Arts Applications) -- and backs up their claim with experiences in Mock Trial and the Innocence Project. Readers are able to see that the Lang Center for Civic and Social Responsibility and the Inside-Out Prison Exchange project are a perfect match for these interests.

Michelle Zhuang

I've been hanging around Swatties for most of my life. I turned six when my sister started Swarthmore, ten when she graduated, and it's been eight years of seeing her and her friends make real-world impact. Diverse in their personalities and professions (entrepreneurs, activists, even admissions officers!), I was struck by the commonalities: socially-conscious, intellectually curious, kind, humor-filled. Swatties are my kindred spirit.

If institutions help shape people, then Swarthmore is the type of institution I know will push me towards my best. Swat challenges its students to explore endless intellectual paths and approach the world with criticality and compassion. Academically, I am drawn to the intersection of engineering and the humanities, and Cognitive Science—with its philosophical underpinnings and real-life applications—gets me most excited. Questions around how we perceive and interact with digital systems or human beings abstracted as avatars— these are the things I've thought about ever since cleaning homes for AirBnB or learning how to code. I want to engage in these questions with professors and peers who get similarly excited by such questions. And if my experience with my sister's friends remains true, these questions and conversations continue well after graduating.

I cannot wait to cultivate my own Swarthmore life soon (up until now, I have jokingly dubbed my experience as "Secondhand Swarthmore"). "Firsthand Swarthmore" doesn't have the same ring as its alliterative cousin, but it will be a story all my own.

Analysis

From this essay, a reader can tell that the author knows what Swarthmore is about. The author describes the "composite Swarthmore student" (socially-conscious, intellectually curious, kind, humor-filled), and recognizes that Swarthmore is a place that encourages its students to "explore endless intellectual paths" and "approach the world with criticality and compassion." The author's own intellectual pursuits, a blend of engineering and humanities, is a great match for this. The sentence about "how we perceive and interact with digital systems or human beings abstracted as avatars" helps explain their interest and gives readers more insight into why they are drawn to cognitive science. This unique interest also helps them stand out. Their essay may have been stronger if they had backed this up with concrete experiences (perhaps the author dove a bit into artificial intelligence or took a class in psychology), and followed this with specific resources at Swat that would match this interest (e.g. Swarthmore's cognitive science major which blends six different disciplines and offers classes like Natural Language Processing and Behavioral Neuroscience). However, the fact that they truly know what Swarthmore is like due to conversations with alumni and that their interests are very interdisciplinary make a strong case that Swarthmore is the right school for this author.

Anonymous

I can confidently say that a Swarthmore education would further foster my enthusiasm for learning.
Throughout my time at Nueva, I've benefited from an
emphasis on learning for its own sake and not for the
grade, and it's clear that Swarthmore cultivates a similar culture with policies such as the pass-fail semester and the elimination of GPAs and class ranks. I can
already see myself as an active participant in Swarthmore's freshman seminars designed to enable student-
led discussions — an atmosphere in which I thrive. The
academic flexibility offered similarly excites me, even if
I can't yet decide if I'm more drawn to pursuing breadth
of knowledge through a course major or depth through
Swarthmore's one of a kind honors program.

As I sat in the cafe on Swarthmore's breathtaking
campus sipping barley soup, I overheard two college students discussing their econometrics projects. It was the
enthusiasm in their voices that made the conversation
stand out as they excitedly murmured about p-values
and time lags. The way academic discourse permeated
the classroom walls and seeped into a casual conversation between two friends brought me back to thoughts
of my own experience geeking out at lunch with my
friends over that cool thesis someone wrote or the elegant new math proof we'd discovered. I detected the
same enthusiasm infused in the APDA debate team when
I met team captains [captain name] and [captain name]
for coffee — it became clear that a love of learning is a
mainstay of the Swarthmore experience.

177

Analysis

This writer's very first sentence exemplifies the liberal arts ethos of Swarthmore -- they are confident that Swarthmore would "foster [their] enthusiasm for learning." They learn for the sake of learning, and they demonstrate open-mindedness (something that Swarthmore Admissions likes to see) when they say, "the academic flexibility offered similarly excites me, even if I can't yet decide if I'm more drawn to pursuing breadth of knowledge through a course major or depth through Swarthmore's one of a kind honors program."

The author goes on to mention conversations with friends, which reinforce that this candidate and Swarthmore are a great match. The student loves to "geek out" over intellectual topics -- something Swatties can't help but do. Also, this person was a debater, so them meeting the APDA debate team captains is a nice addition. Overall, it is very easy to envision this person loving Swarthmore.

Kali Blain

There is a Guyanese saying "My spirit does/doesn't take something," as an explanation of why you do/don't like something. From the moment I stepped on campus, my spirit took Swarthmore. I hadn't been on campus for more than ten minutes and I felt at home. I didn't know anyone, yet I found a group of welcoming Swatties to dine with in Sharples.

From the information session and talking to my tour guide, Wrenn, I realized that Swarthmore isn't just a welcoming environment for studious people, it's also home to the resources that will allow you to make the most of life. The research opportunities available explicitly to undergraduates are unparalleled. At Swarthmore, I would be able to engage in biology research or even a multidisciplinary project that incorporates neuroscience and linguistics.

Swarthmore uses everything it touches as an opportunity to teach and serve. It wasn't enough to have a beautiful, floral campus; they made it an arboretum. Swarthmore uses its proximity to three other excellent schools to form a consortium, expanding its reach beyond its official student body. I want to be a part of a community that encourages that type of thinking. I want to be part of a community that welcomes even strangers with open arms, wishing them success. I don't just want to attend an excellent college; I want to go to a home, and Swarthmore is that home.

Analysis

This essay is strong because it speaks at length

about personal reasons that Swarthmore stands out to the author. One unique aspect of this essay is its introduction, which piques the reader's interest and draws them in. The reader can tell that this person is genuinely impressed by Swarthmore's friendly atmosphere, abundant research opportunities, and community-oriented mindset. The author mentions specific details unique to Swarthmore, like an opportunity to engage in a multidisciplinary project and its consortium with three other schools, showing that the author did their research. This might have been more effective if the author was even more specific, e.g. if they mentioned specific professors they would have liked to do research with, or why they feel the consortium is relevant to their college experience (e.g., do they hope to take classes at Haverford?). However, the fact that this student was able to visit Swathmore's campus and experience it first hand makes their narrative convincing.

Hojune Kim

Professor Gomez greets the class and jumps into a mind-blowing explanation of the concept of continuity. As I copy equations and graphs into my notebook, I scribble down questions to ask during office hours: When does $f(x)=1/x$ turn to zero? Is zero even a number?

Next, on my way to the Sharples, I stroll through the Magill Walk, appreciating the sunlight as it dapples on the sidewalk and shimmers on the green grass. With a bellyful of cheesy fries, I head back up the hill toward Beardsley.

Today's question in the Human Nature class: "Are the mind and the body connected?" A dull headache I have from staying up late tells me to go with Spinoza, but the logical engineer in me nudges me toward Descartes.

Back at the Willets, a few floormates and I continue the philosophical discussion, sharing the thoughts that were too silly or strange for Professor Lorraine. Descartes' theory of the mind and body leads to artificial intelligence, AlphaGo, hard drives that can store consciousness, and, finally, our own cryogenically frozen heads.

This one day from my possible future illustrates why I've chosen Swarthmore. I value the freedom to study both the Sciences and the Humanities in a small community full of intellectually inspired people. I look forward to the man I will become on another day in the future, when I'm graduating at the Scott Outdoor Amphitheater.

Analysis

This essay does a good job of helping the reader imagine this student at Swarthmore. It shows that the author is curious and interested in many things, from complex mathematics topics to philosophical ponderings about consciousness and AI. The "nerdiness" that the author demonstrates is typical of "Swatties." Although this essay is simple, it does a superb job of persuading the reader that the author will be a great fit for Swarthmore.

Anonymous

Last June, my family and I went on a college tour of my dream school (Princeton, of course). But fate would have it that Swarthmore be in the area and that we would have a free morning.

When I arrived on campus, I immediately became angry at your marketing people for planting a forest. It was obviously a ploy to distract me from my blissful thoughts of Princeton. Then you bombarded me with a slew of students and staff whom you intentionally trained to appear passionate, interesting, and friendly. Sly. But don't think I can't see what you're trying to do here.

In the information session I saw how you crafted your academics to rival that of an Ivy League school. Then you added the nasty twist of tailoring it specifically to each individual. You told me I could explore my path freely before declaring my major. Of course, you were exploiting the fact that I was undecided and feeling insecure about it. But then you taunted me with a financial aid package that would make attendance virtually free.

I will not tolerate such coercion! I will not be dissuaded from my dreams of an extremely snobby, academically restrictive, impersonal, forest-less school! I find your superiority offensive, and despite your attacks, I will stubbornly cling to my increasingly-difficult-to-maintain position! I will not apply!

Okay. Fine. I'll apply early decision.

Analysis

This essay is quite unique, especially considering that most "Why Swarthmore" essays are written in a straightforward, somewhat mechanical way. By contrast, this essay is funny and playful, which showcases the student's personality brilliantly (something that is harder to do in a Why Swarthmore essay than in a personal statement), and its whimsical tone and quirkiness helps make the case that they will be a great behavioral fit for Swarthmore. However, this essay does not sacrifice content for entertainment value. It is full of personal reasons why Swarthmore appeals to the author, like that it has a student body full of interesting individuals, or that it has academic requirements made to let students explore their many interests (e.g. pass-fail semester, cross-disciplinary distribution requirements, late declaration of major, and customized special majors).

The essay is also honest and genuine. It indicates their initial attraction to the prestige of schools like Princeton. But it also shows *how* their perspective changed and *why* they ended up finding Swarthmore more appealing. The student makes sure to include all the specific things that stood out to them about Swarthmore. Because of these specific reasons, their love for Swarthmore shows through in a convincing and compelling way.

OUR ESSAYS

More than a Game
Sean Cheng

My mom used to say that if someone plays baseball, they better play to win. I disagreed, but I had little control over her mentality.

As a coach in Challenger, a league for kids with special needs, I refused to be constrained by my mom's limited mindset. Instead, I wanted to share the raw joy of baseball with the players. Since fourth grade, I remember finishing my Little League games and sprinting across the park with my dirt-stained uniform to volunteer at the Challenger games. I went with the players to the snack shack after, munching on Red Vines while talking about our favorite players. We were like a family.

As I grew older, I stepped into a significant leadership role on the team. Directing pre-game batting practice and throwing drills became my responsibilities. After one game, a player named Josh approached and asked, "How can I hit a home run?" I spent half an hour showing him hitting mechanics. Afterward, I thought, "What if I started a camp teaching the players more advanced baseball skills?"

I emailed parents and Challenger coaches all over the county to see if their players would be interested. Requiring volunteers with baseball expertise, I called all my baseball teammates. Most were reluctant, but with the enticing prospect of pepperoni pizza, they agreed. I ended up enrolling ten players and paired up a volunteer with each of them.

I worked closely with a player named Jack. He had

autism and would scream and lash out when his parents left him on the field. Noticing this, I slowly approached Jack, got his glove, and helped slide it onto his small hand. I tried rolling the ball to him, but he kept dropping the glove. Sensing my irritation, Jack started to cry and dashed off the field. Completely fixating on teaching Jack to play catch, I forgot that, for him, even allowing me to help with his glove without running away was already a huge step forward.

I needed a different approach. I put on Jack's glove, bent down into the ready position, and told my teammate to roll me the ball. As I stood up, Jack snatched his glove away from me and thrust it on, ready for the drill.

Baseball is about recognizing the little victories. With Jack, all that mattered was that I celebrated his achievements each step of the way. Seeing Jack's mom happily standing off by the bleachers and chatting with the other parents during practice, I realized that although it may look unremarkable from afar, this was a pivotal moment. For one of the first times ever, she was watching her son play like any other baseball mom. Providing this open and welcoming environment for parents and players is why I started volunteering in the first place.

Heading towards the parking lot after the last practice, Jack's mom approached me. "Thank you for running this camp. Jack really enjoys playing with his teammates each week. He doesn't get the chance to hang out with people other than me very often. Will you do this again next year?" I understood what she meant; team sports marginalize kids like Jack, barring them from participating in most activities. Accessing a supportive team community where Jack felt validated and successful was difficult, but my Challenger camp opened up the door for him and his mom to feel included and not ostracized.

"Of course," I replied. Giving Jack a big high-five, he clutched onto my wrist. He didn't want to leave the baseball diamond. "Hey buddy, I'll see you in a couple months during the spring alright?" He gave out a gleeful scream and ran off.

I've loved playing baseball all my life, but I never found the sport more meaningful than when I volunteered at Challenger. The rush of success in baseball is fleeting, but the impact I have at Challenger is lasting.

One Cent Please
Will Han

I was in big trouble. I had no idea what I had done wrong, but I knew I was in for it. I had just started my first business, and I'd already crafted a high-quality product, acquired loyal customers, and generated revenue. And now, the authorities were after me... I was eight years old.

It all started when I made a story-book, just for fun. But when a friend asked if he could read my literary creation, I was so excited! I said, Yes! One cent please. And boy did my first customer pay a pretty penny (ba dum tss). Soon enough, my books got so popular I was selling them faster than I could even make them. And then it happened. My teacher asked to speak to me after class. I was harshly told to stop selling my books immediately. Why? Because I had broken the rules. So I came out of that meeting as embarrassed, humiliated, and melancholy as my 8-year-old self could feel. And I probably didn't even know how to spell embarrassed, humiliated, or melancholy.

Upon reflection, I've come to believe that my exciting yet humbling elementary school experience illustrates a rather alarming issue in our society — the fact that we students are discouraged from building new ventures of our own and are instead molded to contribute solely to existing businesses. According to Andrew Yang, founder of an entrepreneurial fellowship program called Venture for America, more than half of top college graduates enter one of six pre-established career paths — consulting, finance, law, medicine, graduate school, and

Teach For America — evidence that our most educated and skilled professional workers are no longer trailblazing their own career paths, instead remaining complacent within the well-paved roads society has established for them.

Just a few months ago, I was heading in the same direction: mindlessly following the preordained recipe for success. But, by chance, I stumbled upon a summer entrepreneurship program for high schoolers called Lean Gap, where I spent six weeks in Boston building my own startup. There, I worked with a team of cofounders to ideate, handcraft, and test a product. Together, we identified a problem experienced by all networkers alike: the need to repeatedly purchase unimpressive, unwieldy business cards that wastefully get thrown away and thus harm the environment. With our product, my plan, and my pitch, our team won first place at the program's final pitch competition. Through this perspective-altering experience, I realized that while I *can* excel in working on what others have built, there is another way: I can build something entirely new. And it is not against the rules.

Since the start of Lean Gap, our team has gotten an article on the LA Times High School Insider, pitched to Goldman Sachs, sponsored a hackathon (HackThe6ix), and earned a grant of $500 from an investment firm. With each step, I encountered a fear of venturing into the unknown. But as I overcame each hurdle, I realized that I and anyone else can not only conquer these fears but reach unimaginable heights — if we are willing. That if I, at eight years old and then again at sixteen years old, learned to unlock my creative potential, then there is nothing stopping me from encouraging everyone around me to do the same. Whether by crafting my experiences and insights into an Original Oratory for Speech and Debate or by researching for a comprehensive proposal to replace styrofoam trays at my high school, I've taken steps toward fostering a community of builders where risk-taking, problem-solving, and idea-generating are appreciated and encouraged. For the rest of my student career and beyond, my aim is to continue inspiring others by leading the way in rejecting contentment with blind conformity. With this grassroots approach, I can ensure that future 3rd graders with the entrepreneurial spirit will not be dissuaded but supported by their transformed communities.

TRANSFER ESSAY

Chayanne Petit

1. Swarthmore students are socially aware in both a broad, global context as well as an interpersonal, community context. They approach problems with intentionality, and they often contemplate their place in the world. Given this tendency we would like to know, "What keeps you up at night?"

One day I hope to work either in international healthcare as a physician for a non-profit organization such as Médecins Sans Frontières or in the legal field as a lawyer and advocate for disenfranchised groups. Through these careers, I want to help others and have a significant and positive impact on their lives. Although I want to use my privilege meaningfully, it does not change the tremendous amount of privilege I have. I am white, educated, middle class, and have a stable home life. How do these privileges impact my place in our world and in these career fields? What are the ethical implications joining the international healthcare field? Will I significantly improve the quality of life of others, or because of my race and nationality will I further an agenda of neocolonialism? If I practice environmental law to protect minority groups from environmental racism, will I be helping these groups sustainably? How do I avoid contributing to 'whitesplaining' and paternal racism?

I believe dedicating my life in service to others, and especially in service to those who do not benefit from the same privileges as me, would be the most fulfilling use of my time. However, I wrestle with finding a balance between my dreams and good intentions with what is morally and ethically right. I need to walk the line keeping me on the path of meaningfully, positively, and sustainably helping others without unintentionally crossing into the territory of abusing and losing sight of the gravity of my privilege.

2. Please write about why you are interested in applying to and attending Swarthmore. You should also address how you anticipate your experience at Swarthmore to be different from your current institution or circumstance.

Two years ago, I described my dream college to a friend and he told me that it sounded exactly like Swarthmore College. I quickly found he was absolutely right. In Swarthmore College I see the promise of a small, diverse community of high-achieving individuals sharing a common goal. It is not about mounting a degree on the wall, but about developing into individuals we cannot even fathom becoming. Aided by professors and peers, every student embarks on a journey of growth into self actualized, eloquent people capable of enacting significant change in our world.

The diversity of Swarthmore's student body is crucial not because of its potential use in recruitment literature, but because the privilege of having such a community is celebrated. Swarthmore holds students to an incredibly high standard; there is faith that every student is capable and worthy of reaching their full potential. Students are not stifled by the stress of earning perfect grades because the relative insignificance of a number compared to the importance of engaging in risk and inquiry is acknowledged. Accordingly, students are allowed to withhold the grades of two classes they take.

Two years ago, I shared my wildest dreams not knowing that my words constitute reality in Swarthmore College. Today I am in awe knowing there is a chance I can finish my undergraduate career in my own utopia.

3. Provide a statement that addresses your reasons for transferring and the objectives you hope to achieve. You can type directly into the box, or you can paste text from another source.

I moved away from home when I was just fifteen years old to attend a residential high school. I thought I would find an incredible level of independence, but instead I found a family of students and faculty who nurtured my personal and academic growth. My teachers never answered questions, but instead directed them back to me and encouraged my formation of unique conclusions. In fact, my organic chemistry final consisted of being handed a vial of powder and told, "Find out what it is."

I took advantage of abundant opportunities, from conducting engineering research about affordable ways of distilling water to tutoring refugee students. I aspired to live my school's motto of becoming an individual who will "advance the human condition." This has informed my goals of becoming either a physician for an organization such as Médecins Sans Frontières or an environmental lawyer tackling environmental racism. I know my purpose is to use my privilege meaningfully to address social inequalities. However, I need my time three years as an undergraduate student to be spent in a community that will guide my journey. It takes a village, and I believe mine is in Swarthmore, Pennsylvania.

I decided to attend Michigan State University (MSU), a striking contrast from my otherwise uniform lineup of small, liberal arts colleges, for financial and family reasons. However, I hoped that in a school with such academically vast resources, I would find my niche and I was ready to advocate for myself. My classmates at MSU are good, kind people, but they have reasons for attending a higher institution different than mine. They often do not match my passion and investment in furthering my knowledge of the world and applying it in meaningful ways, simply because we have different outlooks and goals.

When I realized in September that my original enrollment in Chinese 201 did not align with my skill level, I negotiated to advance to Chinese 301. To fulfill my desire for interdisciplinarity, I took classes far outside my Chemistry major, such as Readings in Chicano and Latino Literature. Because I missed the lively debates crucial to the study of literature, I collaborated with my teacher to meet bi-weekly and further discuss class materials. However despite my best efforts, the culture of MSU remained incompatible with my personal and educational goals. The sheer size of the campus continued to imbue the feeling of impersonality and ironically, loneliness. My classmates often do not match my passion for collaboration, inquiry, and interdisciplinarity because we have different aims in attending a university.

Over the past six months, I have realized that I long

to spend my next three years as a member of a close-knit community; where high academic standards and inter-disciplinarity are intrinsic to the fabric of the institution. There I will be encouraged to pursue a wide variety of interests. The pursuit of these interests will serve not to distract me, but rather to better inform my decision about what kind of career suits me best. I want to sit in class knowing that I am surrounded by individuals with different paths in life who are equally curious, eager for collaboration, and ready to engage in active learning. The end goal of my peers will not be limited to the obtaining of degree, but our development and growth into eloquent, considerate, and capable citizens of the world. I am often most inspired by my peers, and I am looking for an environment where my high-achieving peers will be a source of inspiration nonpareil. Finally, I want to look to the front of the classroom to a professor who knows me by name and is ready and willing to invest in me. I am confident that Swarthmore College will provide all this and more.

ACKNOWLEDGEMENT

Thank you to all the students who contributed their essays to this book. We also want to thank Maria Aghazarian with all of our hearts for all her help and support. This book would not have been possible without her. Thank you, Jim Bock and Andrew Moe from the Swarthmore Admissions Office for being an incredibly helpful resource and for writing the Q&A Chapter in this book. Thanks also to Skylar Thoma and Ashley Pyon for their contributions, which helped us tremendously with writing the "Your Written Tour of Swarthmore" Chapter. Thank you to Janine Chan and Roma Bedekar for your contributions as well.

Made in the USA
Middletown, DE
11 October 2022

12456849R00115